The De~~~~

– A Complete Anthology of the Dog –

1860-1940

ISBN No.
978-14455-2593-8 (Paperback)
978-14455-2713-0 (Hardback)

British Library Cataloguing-in-Publication Data
A catalogue record for this book is available from
the British Library

VDB

www.vintagedogbooks.com

Contents

Containing chapters from the following sources:

THE DEERHOUND.

This dog is now more ornamental than useful, his former trade of retrieving wounded deer in Scotland being often entrusted to colleys, whole or half-bred, and cross-bred dogs of various kinds, but in the south his grand size and outline make him a great favourite with country gentlemen, and more especially with the ladies of their families. For this fashion Sir Walter Scott with his Ban and Buskar, immortalised in "Waverley," is mainly responsible, as with the Dandie Dinmonts in "Guy Mannering."

There is no doubt that the Scotch deerhound and the thorough Scotch greyhound were identical in shape, and could scarcely be distinguished by good judges, and even by them only when at work, the deerhound galloping with his head considerably higher than the greyhound. *Pari passu* with the disappearance of the rough greyhound has been the rarity of the deerhound in modern days, the former being displaced by the smooth breed, and the latter by various crosses, *e.g.*, that between the foxhound and greyhound advocated by Mr. Scrope; the mastiff and greyhound cross of the Earl of Stamford, and all sorts of crosses between the colley and greyhound, rough as well as smooth, as mentioned above. In the present day pure deerhounds *kept for the retrieving of deer* are comparatively rare, and I believe even those in Her Majesty's kennel are not used for that purpose. Hence it is idle to attempt to describe this dog solely from the deer-stalker's point of view, and he must be estimated rather from an artistic standpoint, in which capacity he rivals, and perhaps surpasses, all his brethren, having the elegant frame of the greyhound united with a rough shaggy coat, which takes off the hardness of outline complained of by the lovers of the picturesque as attaching to the English "longtail." Still, though the deerhound of modern days is to be considered as a companionable dog rather than as a deer retriever, as he has always hitherto been regarded as coming under the latter category, and is

1

so classed in all our shows, I shall not attempt to displace him from his old time-honoured position. As a companion he must depend for a good character on his ornamental appearance, rather than on his utility as a protector of dames, in which capacity he is quite useless as compared with the mastiff, St. Bernard, or Newfoundland. He is not so quarrelsome as the colley, but when attacked defends himself with great power, quickness, and courage. His chief defect as a companion is his proneness to chase any moving object, and he will even pick up little dogs, especially if they attempt to run away from him; and if not broken early from this habit, he often occasions trouble to his owner. On the other hand, he is seldom offensive to strangers, but he does not take to children, and is seldom to be trusted with them. Unless well broken, he will chase hares and rabbits, and of course deer, and on that account he should not be taken into deer parks or game preserves by those who are not sure of being able to control him.

The disproportion between the sexes is greater than in any other breed of dogs, the average difference in height in the same litter being often from five to six inches.

When this dog is slipped at a wounded deer, he pursues it either by scent or sight, the latter being, of course, used in preference, but the nose being lowered for the trail the moment the deer is lost to the eye. In hunting the trail, however hot and fresh, the deerhound does not throw his tongue out as a rule, though, as is the case even with some of the highest bred greyhounds, occasionally a low whimper is heard. When a stag stands at bay, the dog opens with a loud sharp bark, and continues till his master appears to give the *coup de grace*, unless his quarry is sufficiently exhausted by loss of blood to permit his pinioning him; but a stag in possession of his full powers is beyond the reach of any dog from the front, and a well-bred deerhound does not make the attempt unless he sees an opening from behind. A cross with the bulldog was tried some years ago in order to give courage, which it did; but it also gave the peculiar bulldog tendency to go at the head of the deer, and led to the loss of so many valuable animals that it was abandoned.

The numerical value of the points of this dog is as follows:

POINTS OF THE DEERHOUND.

	Value.		Value.		Value.
Skull	10	Chest and shoulders...	10	Legs and quarters ...	7½
Nose and jaws	5	Back and back ribs ...	10	Feet	7½
Ears and eyes	5	Elbows and stifles......	10	Colour and coat	10
Neck	10	Symmetry and quality	10	Tail	5
	30		**40**		**30**

Grand Total 100.

1. In *skull* (value 10) the deerhound resembles the large coarse greyhound, it being long and moderately wide, especially between the ears. There is a very slight rise at the eyebrows so as to take off what would otherwise be a straight line from tip of nose to occiput. The upper surface is level in both directions.

2

2. *Nose and jaws* (value 5).—The jaws should be long and the teeth level and strong. Nostrils open but not very wide, and the end pointed and black; cheeks well clothed with muscle, but the bone under the eye neither prominent nor hollow.

3. *Ears and eyes* (value 5).—The *ears* should be small and thin and carried a trifle higher than those of the smooth greyhound, but should turn over at the tips. Pricked ears are sometimes met with, as in the rough greyhound, but they are not correct. They should be thinly fringed with hair at the edges only; that on their surfaces should be soft and smooth. Eyes full and dark hazel, sometimes by preference blue.

4. The *neck* (value 10) should be long enough to allow the dog to stoop to the scent at a fast pace, but not so long and tapering as the greyhound. It is usually also a little thinner than the corresponding part in the dog.

5. *Chest and shoulders* (value 10).—The chest is deep rather than wide, and in its general formation it resembles that of the greyhound, being shaped with great elegance, and at the same time so that the shoulders can play freely on its sides. The girth of a full sized dog deerhound should be at least two inches greater than his height, often an inch or two more, but a round unwieldy chest is not to be desired, even if girthing well, shoulders long, oblique, and muscular.

6. *Back and back ribs* (value 10).—Without a powerful loin a large dog like this cannot sustain the sweeping stride which he possesses, and therefore a deep and wide development of muscle filling up the space between wide back ribs and somewhat ragged hips is the *desideratum*. A good loin should measure 25 or 26 inches in show condition. The back ribs are often rather shallow, but they must be wide, or what is called "well sprung," and the loin should be arched, drooping to the root of the tail.

7. *Elbows and stifles* (value 10), if well placed, give great liberty of action, and the contrary if they are confined by being too close together. These points should therefore be carefully examined. The elbows must be well let down to give length to the true arm, and should be quite straight, that is, neither turned in or out. The stifles should be wide apart and set well forward to give length to the upper thigh. Many otherwise well-made deerhounds are very straight in their stifles.

8. The *high symmetry* (value 10) of this dog is essential to his position as a companionable dog, and it is therefore estimated accordingly. *Quality* is also to be regarded as of great importance.

9. *Legs and quarters* (value 7½).—Great bone and muscle must go to the formation of these parts, and the bones must be well put together at the knees and hocks, which should be long and well developed. The quarters are deep but seldom wide, and there is often a considerable slope to the tail. Some of the most successful dogs lately exhibited, and notably Mr. Musters's Torunn and Mr. Beasley's Countess, have been nearly straight backed, but this shape is not approved of by deerstalkers.

10. The *feet* (value 7½) should be well arched in the toes and catlike—a wide spreading foot is often met with, but should be specially condemned.

11. *Colour and coat* (value 10).—The *colours* most in request are dark blue,

3

fawn, grizzle, and brindled, the latter with a more or less tint of blue. The fawn should have the tips of the ears dark, but some otherwise good fawns are pale throughout. The grizzle generally has a decided tint of blue in it. White is to be avoided either on breast or toes, but it should not disqualify a dog. The *coat* (value 5) is coarser on the back than elsewhere, and by many good judges it is thought that even on the back it should be intermediate between silk and wool, and not the coarse hair often met with; and there is no doubt that both kinds of coat are found in some of the best strains. The whole body is clothed with a rough coat sometimes amounting to shagginess, that of the muzzle is longer in proportion than elsewhere, but the moustache should not be wiry, and should stand out in irregular tufts. There should be no approach to feather on the legs as in the setter, but their inside should be hairy.

12. The *tail* (value 5) should be long and gently curved, without any twist. It should be thinly clothed with hair only.

The most successful exhibitor at our shows for the last ten years is Mr. Chaworth Musters, of Kirk Langton, with his two Torunns, father and son. The old dog was of the Monzie strain, and was the sire of several prize winners, including Brenda, Hylda, Meg, Mr. Parkes's Bevis, Hilda and Teeldar, the younger Torunn, and Mr. Fitt's Bruce, all which (except the first two) were from sister to Morni, his chief competitor on the show bench. Next to him comes Mr. J. N. Beasley, of Brampton House, Northampton, with Alder and Countess, both with unknown pedigrees; and third, very nearly approaching them indeed, is Mr. Hickman, of Birmingham, whose Morni alone has taken eight first or champion prizes, whereas Old Torunn stopped short at five. Countess was undoubtedly, in my opinion, the most beautiful deerhound I ever saw, and quite unapproached by either dog or bitch; Mr. Allen's fawn bitch Hylda (the dam of Morni), who took the second prize to her at Birmingham in 1867, being also a splendid specimen of the breed. The latter was by a dog in Her Majesty's kennels. Bran, whose portrait is retained as showing well all the points of the deerhound, was by Mr. Stewart Hodgson's Oscar, son of a dog belonging to Colonel Lennard, of Wickham-cross, and of the breed of Mr. M'Kenzie, of Applecross, Ross-shire. His dam was Mr. Cole's (Her Majesty's keeper) Hylda, by his Old Kieldar out of Tank; Old Kieldar by Hector, a dog presented to Her Majesty by Mr. Campbell, of Monzie.

The measurement of Bran was as follows: From nose to setting on of tail, 47 inches; tail, 22 inches; height, 32 inches; length of head, 12 inches; circumference of head, $17\frac{1}{4}$ inches; round arm at elbow, $9\frac{1}{2}$ inches; girth at chest, $33\frac{1}{4}$ inches; girth at loin, 24 inches; round thigh, $17\frac{1}{4}$ inches; round lower thigh hock, 7 inches; knee, 7 inches.

THE DEERHOUND.

BY G. A. GRAHAM, DURSLEY.

THE transition from the Irish Wolfhound to the Deerhound is easy and natural, as in the latter we unmistakably have the descendant of the former. The subject is, moreover, the more easily treated of, as we have many excellent specimens of the Deerhound before us. Indeed, the examples of the breed now scattered in considerable profusion throughout the land are far finer dogs than those of which much boast was made forty years ago.

The earliest records we have of the Deerhound as a distinct breed are, it is believed, given to us by Pennant, who, in his tour in 1769, says:—"I saw also at Castle Gordon a true Highland Greyhound, which has become very scarce. It was of a large size, strong, deep-chested, and covered with very long and rough hair. This kind was in great vogue in former days, and used in vast numbers at the magnificent stag-chases by the powerful chieftains."

Then Macpherson, in his professed translation of Ossian's poems (1773), gives testimony—worthless, no doubt, as regards the Irish Wolfhound, but having a decided value when the Deerhound is considered, as it was almost a certainty that he wrote his descriptions from the living animal. The following extracts will be found of interest :—"Fingal agreed to hunt in the Forest of Sledale, in company with the Sutherland chief his contemporary, for the purpose of trying the comparative merits of their dogs. Fingal brought his celebrated dog Bran to Sutherland, in order to compete with an equally famous dog belonging to the Sutherland chief, and the only one in the country supposed to be a match for him. The approaching contest between these fine animals created great interest. White-breasted Bran was superior to the whole of Fingal's other dogs, even to the 'surly strength of Luath;' but the Sutherland dog—known by the full-sounding name of Phorp—was incomparably the best and most powerful dog that ever eyed a deer in his master's forests."

Phorp was black in colour, and his points are thus described :—

> " ' Two yellow feet such as Bran had,
> Two black eyes,
> And a white breast,
> A back narrow and fair,
> As required for hunting,
> And two erect ears of a dark red-brown.'

"Towards the close of the day, after some severe runs—which, however, still left the comparative merits of the two dogs a subject of hot dispute—Bran and Phorp were brought front to front to prove their courage; and they were no sooner untied than they sprang at each other and fought desperately. Phorp seemed about to overcome Bran, when his master, the Sutherland chief, unwilling that either of them should be killed, called out—'Let each

5

of us take away his dog.' Fingal objected to this, whereupon the Sutherland chief said with a taunt that it was now evident that the Fingalians did not possess a dog that could match with Phorp.

"Angered and mortified, Fingal immediately extended his 'venomous paw,' as it is called (for the tradition represents him as possessing supernatural power), and with one hand he seized Phorp by the neck, and with the other—which was a charmed and destructive one—he tore out the brave animal's heart. This adventure occurred at a place near the March, between the parishes of Clyne and Wildonan, still called 'Leck na Con' (the stone of the dogs), there having been placed a large stone on the spot where they fought. The ground over which Fingal and the Sutherland chief hunted that day is called 'Dirri-leck-Con.' Bran suffered so severely in the fight that he died in Glen Loth before leaving the forest, and was buried there; a huge cairn was heaped over him, which still remains, and is known by the name of 'Cairn Bran.'"

Our next authority is Bewick (1792). Having described the Irish Wolfhound, he then goes on to say:—"Next to this in size and strength is the Scottish Highland Greyhound or Wolfdog, which was formerly used by the chieftains of that country in their grand hunting parties. One of them, which we saw some years ago, was a large, powerful, fierce-looking dog; its ears were pendulous, and its eyes half hid in the hair; its body was strong and muscular, and covered with harsh, wiry, reddish hair, mixed with white."

The "Encyclopædia Britannica" (1797) says:—"The variety called the Highland Gre-hound, and now become very scarce, is of great size, strong, deep-chested, and covered with long rough hair. This kind was much esteemed in former days, and used in great numbers by the powerful chieftains in their magnificent hunting matches. It had as sagacious nostrils as the Bloodhound, and was as fierce."

There is no allusion to the Deerhound in the "Sportsman's Cabinet," published in 1803; and, curiously enough, but little information regarding him from the beginning of this century up to about 1838, when McNeill wrote regarding him and the Irish Wolfhound in Scrope's book. That the breed *was* kept up in some families will be presently shown— in one case it was claimed that it had been in the owner's family for at least one hundred years. However, be that as it may, we have few, if any, reliable accounts of this dog until McNeill wrote. That gentleman, writing in 1838, says:—"It is not a little remarkable that the species of dog which has been longest in use in this country for the purposes of the chase should be that which is least known to the present generation of naturalists and sportsmen."

Mr. McNeill takes exception to the crosses which had been resorted to by "Glengarry" and others for the purpose of giving increased vigour and size to a breed then rapidly degenerating; but there seems every reason to suppose that had it not been for these judicious crosses the breed would have been almost extinct: at any rate, it would still further have deteriorated. It is very evident, from the following description of Captain McNeill's Buskar, that the Deerhound of forty years ago was a very inferior animal in size and power to the Deerhound of the present day, though possibly he equalled him in courage and speed. Buskar was a sandy-coloured dog, with dark ears, which were nearly erect when excited. He stood 28 inches in height, girthed 32 inches round the chest, and

6

weighed 85 lbs. The hair was hard, not very rough, wiry only on head and legs. He was pupped in 1832, and was looked upon as a remarkably staunch and useful dog. McNeill considered that the purest dogs of his time were sandy or fawn in colour, and hard coated, but he also tells us that "there are dogs in the Lochabar district which are dark in colour and have a softer coat."

From "Chambers's Information for the People," published in 1842, the following extract is taken :—" The Scottish Highland Greyhound will either hunt in packs or singly. He is an animal of great size and strength, and at the same time very swift of foot. In size he equals, if not excels, the Irish Greyhound. His head is long and the nose sharp; his ears short and somewhat pendulous at the tips ; his eyes are brilliant and very penetrating, and half-concealed by the long crisp hair which covers his face and whole body. He is remarkable for the depth of his chest, and tapers gradually towards the loins, which are of great strength and very muscular; his back is slightly arched ; his hind quarters are powerfully formed, and his limbs strong and straight. The possession of these combined qualities particularly fit him for long endurance in the chase. His usual colour is reddish sand-colour mixed with white ; his tail is long and shaggy, which he carries high like the Staghound, although not quite so erect. He is a noble dog, and was used by the Scottish Highland chieftains in their great hunting parties, and is supposed to have descended in regular succession from the dogs of Ossian."

St. John, in his "Wild Sports of the Highlands," published in 1846, says :—" The breed of Deerhounds, which had nearly become extinct, or at any rate was very rare a few years ago, has now become comparatively plentiful in all the Highland districts, owing to the increased extent of the preserved forests and the trouble taken by the different proprietors and renters of mountain shootings, who have collected and bred this noble race of dogs, regardless of expense and difficulties. The prices given for a well-bred and tried dog of this kind are so large that it repays the cost and trouble of rearing him. Fifty guineas is not an unusual price for a first-rate dog, while from twenty to thirty are frequently given for a tolerable one."
"Started this morning at daybreak with Donald and Malcolm Mohr, as he is called (*Anglicé* Malcolm the Great, or Big Malcolm), who had brought his two Deerhounds Bran and Oscar, to show me how they could kill a stag. The dogs were perfect : Bran an immense but beautifully-made dog of a light colour, with black eyes and muzzle, his ears of a dark brown, soft and silky as a lady's hand, the rest of his coat being wiry and harsh, though not exactly rough and shaggy, like his comrade Oscar, who was long-haired and of a darker brindle colour, with sharp long muzzle, but the same soft ears as Bran, which, by-the-bye, is a distinctive mark of high breeding in these days."

The "Museum of Animated Nature," published in 1848—50, has the following :—"In Scotland and Ireland there existed in very ancient times a noble breed of Greyhound, used for the chase of the wolf and the deer, which appears to us to be the pure source of our present breed ; it is quite as probable that the Mâtin is a modification of the ancient Greyhound of Europe, represented by the Irish Greyhound or Wolfdog, as that it is the source of that fine breed. Few, we believe, of the old Irish Greyhound exist. In Scotland the old Deerhound may still be met with, and though it exceeds the

7

common Greyhound in size and strength, it is said to be below its ancient standard. With the extirpation of the wolf, the necessity of keeping up the breed to the highest perfection ceased. The hair is wiry, the chest remarkable for volume, and the limbs long and muscular."

Youatt furnishes us with this description of the Deerhound:—"The Highland Greyhound, or Deerhound, is the larger, stronger, and fiercer dog, and may readily be distinguished from the Lowland Scotch Greyhound by its pendulous and generally darker ears, and by the length of hair which almost covers his face. Many accounts have been given of the perfection of its scent, and it is said to have followed a wounded deer during two successive days. He is usually two inches taller than the Scotch Greyhound. The head is carried particularly high, and gives to the animal a noble appearance. The limbs are exceedingly muscular; his back beautifully arched. The tail is long and curved, but assumes the form of almost a straight line when he is much excited. The only fault these dogs have is their occasional ill-temper or ferocity; but this does not extend to the owner and his family."

Richardson, writing about 1848, gives the following regarding the Deerhound:—"The Highland Deerhound presents the general aspect of a Highland Greyhound, especially in all the points on which speed and power depend; but he is built more coarsely and altogether on a larger and more robust scale. The shoulder is also more elevated, the neck thicker, head and muzzle coarser, and the bone more massive. The Deerhound stands from twenty-eight to thirty inches in height at the shoulders; his coat is rough and the hair strong; colour usually iron-grey, sandy, yellow, or white; all colours should have the muzzle and tips of the ears black; a tuft or pencil of dark hair on the tip of the ear is a proof of high blood. This is a very powerful dog, equally staunch and faithful; and when the Scottish mountains swarmed with stags and roes, it was held in high estimation, as being capable of following the deer over surfaces too rough and fatiguing for the ordinary hounds of the low country. The general aspect of the Highland hound is commanding and fierce. His head is long, and muzzle rather sharp; his ears pendulous, but not long; his eyes large, keen, and penetrating, half concealed among the long, stiff, and bristly hair with which his face is covered; his body is very strong and muscular, deep-chested, tapering towards the loins, and his back slightly arched. His hind quarters are furnished with large prominent muscles, and his legs are long, strong-boned, and straight—a combination of qualities which gives him that speed and long endurance for which he is so eminently distinguished. This is the dog formerly used by the Highland chieftains of Scotland in their grand hunting parties, and is in all probability the same noble dog used in the time of Ossian."

The last author treating of the Deerhound that will be alluded to is "Idstone," who brought out his useful book on "The Dog," in the year 1872; but as a considerable portion of the information in the article on the Deerhound therein contained was furnished by the present writer, he will embody it in this treatise as he proceeds. At the same time a few extracts which he cannot lay claim to will not be out of place.

"Until within the last few years the breed was very scarce, for they were kept by the few men who owned the Scotch forests or wide wild tracts of deer-park in the less populated parts of England.

"The fault of the present day with Deerhounds is certainly the short body, the thick, and, as the ignorant consider, the necessarily strong jaw, and the open, loose, flat foot. In proportion to the weight, the foot 'goes,' or deteriorates, and the strain upon a Deerhound's foot at speed amongst stones and boulders, 'in view,' and roused to desperation, is greater than that imposed upon any other domesticated animal. No dog but the 'rough-footed Scot' could stand it.

"The Deerhound is one of the oldest breeds we have. I should be inclined to think that it is an *imported* breed. He is probably identical with the 'Strong Irish Grey-hound' mentioned as employed in the Earl of Mar's chase of the red deer, in 1618, by Taylor, in his 'Pennilesse Pilgrimage.'

The oldest strain known is, without doubt, that of the late Mr. Menzies, of Chesthill, on Loch Tay. It is claimed, with every just right, no doubt, that this strain has been in the hands of Mr. Menzies' ancestors for something like eighty to ninety years. Whether it still exists in its integrity the writer is unable to say decidedly; but he is under the impression that as a distinct strain it has disappeared, though there are several dogs in existence that inherit the blood, and that not very distantly. It was asserted that during the time the breed had been in the Menzies family it had only thrice been recruited from outside! Mr. Potter, M.P. for Rochdale, then residing at Pitnacree, Perthshire, had, in 1860, a dog, called Oscar, from Mr. Menzies, and subsequently a bitch, called Lufra, from him. From these many puppies were bred, and given away by him with a liberal hand. A bitch was given to the late Dr. Cox, of Manchester, and from her and Dr. Cox's Ross (by Duke of Devonshire's Roswell, out of Sir R. Peel's Brenda) was bred Buz, the property of Mr. R. Hood Wright, of Birkby Hall, Cark, Carnforth. From this bitch Mr. Wright bred, by a dog (Oscar) of the Duke of Sutherland's breed, his celebrated prize-taker Bevis. It may be here mentioned that Oscar was sold to Prince Albert Solms, of Braunfels, and went to Germany some years ago. The brother to Mr. Cox's Lufra was presented to Menotti Garibaldi, for hunting the mouflon in Sardinia. Oscar, Mr Potter's original Chesthill dog, was given to the late Lord Breadalbane; and descendants of Oscar and Lufra were presented by Mr. Potter to Mr. Cunliffe Brooks, M.P., who, it is believed, has the breed now—indeed, the finest dog at Balmoral lately was one of Mr. C. Brooks's breeding. Mr. Hickman, of Westfield, Selly Hill, near Birmingham, exhibited two brindle dogs at the last Birmingham Show, got by his celebrated Morni out of Garry, by Chesthill Ossian—Lufra. Garry is the property of Mr. Spencer Lucy, of Charlcote. Next to the Chesthill strain, the earliest that the writer knows of is that of Mr. Morrison, of Scalascraig, Glenelg. Mr. John Cameron, of Moy, a farmer residing near Fortwilliam, formerly in service with "Glengarry" as keeper, can remember this breed as far back as 1830. From Bran, a celebrated dog belonging to Mr. Morrison (by him given to McNiel of Colonsay, and afterwards presented by McNiel to Prince Albert), was descended Torrom, the grandsire of Gillespie's celebrated Torrom. The strain of McNiel of Colonsay was known about 1832, and from his strain many of our modern dogs claim descent. The late Mr. Bateson, of Cambusmere in Sutherlandshire, deceased early in 1879, became possessed of a brace of this breed about 1845, named Torrish and Morven. These dogs were sketched by Landseer, the original being now in the hands of Mr. Bateson's family; and he considered them at the time the finest Deerhounds he had ever

9

seen. They were two magnificent dogs, both very rough and of great height and power : Morven reddish in colour, Torrish, darker greyish-brown; Torrish the thickest and biggest in bone, Morven the highest. It is believed this dog left no progeny, though there is an old dog, belonging to the Marquis of Bristol, at Ickworth Park, who is descended in a straight line from his brother Torrish. This dog, Giaour, was bred by Mr. John Bateson, brother to the late Mr. Bateson of Cambusmere, and to him the writer is indebted for all the information regarding these dogs. The breed was entirely in his and his brother's hands from 1845 to the present time, so there can be no doubt regarding its authentic character. The McNiel strain was also owned by Mr. Meredith of Torrish, Sutherlandshire. From a bitch bred by Mr. McNiel, and owned by Mr. Meredith, the Duke of Sutherland's Loyal was bred. Loyal was the dam of the dog Oscar, purchased by Prince Solms, Mr. Cameron's (of Lochiel) Pirate being the sire. As far as can be ascertained, the McNiel dogs in their earliest form were a smaller dog than the present animal, and hardly so rough in the coat, not much exceeding in size the dog, now nearly extinct, that was known as the Scotch Greyhound.

Sir John McNiel was kind enough to furnish the writer, in 1868, with the following information about his breed in later times :—

"The largest and finest dog I ever bred or ever saw was my Oscar. His speed was such that in a straight run he was never beaten by any dog, rough or smooth; and in his best running condition he weighed ninety-four pounds."

From this it will be seen that the McNiel strain had gained both in size and weight since the time Buskar was looked upon as such a wonder.

Another celebrated strain was owned by a Scottish nobleman up to within the last twenty-six years, since which period he has given them up; but some of the blood has passed into other hands, and has been infused in and incorporated with our present strains. The following information furnished by him will be read with much interest :—

"I have never had in my possession a dog above 31 inches. Black Bran, so called to distinguish him from my famous Bran, stood 31 inches in height, and at eighteen months old measured 33½ inches round the chest. He was a first-rate dog. I have seen a dog 34 inches in height, but he was an ill-shaped and utterly useless animal. Sir St. George Gore's Gruim was, I believe, about 32 or 33 inches in height, well-shaped, and a very excellent dog. Gruim was about the year 1843-44, Black Bran about 1850-51, at their best. Bran (the famous) was 29 inches high, and measured 31½ inches round the chest. In shape he was long and low, and so evenly made that he looked much smaller than he really was. He was dark brown at the top of his head—something of the colour of a yell-hind; ears coal black; muzzle black, with a little patch in front of the under-jaw—something like the lips of a roe; back, sides, quarters, and outside of legs yellowish-fawn—deepening in winter time, when his coat was longer, into a sort of yellowish rusty-grey; tail just tipped with white; head quite smooth to behind the ears; ears quite smooth and velvety; coat over body and sides not very long, very harsh and wiry; legs and feet quite smooth; coat, in winter, about three inches long. Bran was at his best about 1844-45. He was entered to his first stag at nine months old (too early), and killed his last stag at nine years old. His greatest feat was the killing of two unwounded stags single-handed in about three-quarters of an hour. The first bore 10 points; the second 11. The pure breed was at one time confined to a very few different kennels. I think my own, and those

10

DEERHOUND.

of Mr. McNiel, of Colonsay, the late Mr. Stewart Menzies, of Chesthill, and one or two others, were the only gentlemen's kennels in which it was preserved. There were also three or four large farmers in various parts of the country who knew the value of the true breed, and took great pains to preserve the pure strain ; but since the great increase of deer forests, in most of which the use of Deerhounds is strictly prohibited, the breeding of these dogs has been very much discontinued, and it is now exceedingly difficult to find one worth anything. Colonel Inge and Lord H. Bentinck have both got my blood. I do not like the Glengarry blood. It was spoilt many years ago by old Glengarry crossing his dogs with the Bloodhound."

The Marquis of Breadalbane, many years ago, owned a famous strain of Deerhounds. They were kept at the Black Mount Forest Lodge. As many as fifty or sixty were kept. A dog called King of the Forest was of extraordinary size. He was an ancestor of a well-known modern prize-taker, also of great size, called Torrom, bred and first exhibited by Mr. Cameron of Lochiel.

The late Sir St. George Gore owned some very fine Deerhounds ; one of his is stated to have stood 32 inches. A young dog shown by him at Birmingham, about thirteen years ago, stood nearly 31 inches, and weighed 105 lbs.; a remarkably fine, well-shaped dog, of a cream colour, but nearly smooth-coated. A bitch, Corrie, brindled, was also large, but poor in coat.

The strain of the late Lord H. Bentinck was very similar to Sir St. G. Gore's—indeed, they bred together for years, and the consequence was that Lord Henry's strain was sadly devoid of coat. A bitch he owned, called Ferret, of McNiel of Colonsay's breed, was smooth, and from her, in all probability, the want of coat was introduced ; indeed, in many of the older strains the coat would appear to have been decidedly indifferent, to say the least of it. Lord Henry's Fingal, considered by him to be one of his very best, was a large red dog, almost smooth. From a bitch of this breed, called Carrac, at one time owned by the writer, many of our best modern dogs are descended. At Lord Henry's death his dogs were sold at Edinburgh in 1871, realising by no means large prices.

Some extremely fine Deerhounds were owned many years ago by the late Duke of Leeds.

Mr. Campbell of Monzie, Perthshire, had a very pure breed of Deerhounds about fifteen or twenty years ago. " Lochiel," speaking of them, says :—" I doubt if any Deerhounds except Mr. Campbell's of Monzie are quite pure. There were very few of them left at his death. His was the best and purest blood in the North." From his dog Grumach Mr. Cameron's Pirate and Torrom were bred.

Lieutenant-Colonel Inge of Thorpe for many years bred Deerhounds of remarkably good descent ; but he ceased to do so about 1862, when he sent sixteen to be sold at Aldridge's. They fetched prices ranging from 15 to 60 guineas. His celebrated old dog Valiant was bought in at a large figure. They were all well-made dogs and well covered with rough hair, but were not remarkable for size. Colonel Inge had the honour of winning the first prize with Valiant at the first dog show ever held at Birmingham in 1861. He was a very rough brindle dog of lengthy make. Valiant's pedigree was given as by Lord Saltoun's famous Bran out of Seaforth's Vengeance, and he was presented to Colonel Inge when a puppy.

The late Mr. John Cole, for many years head keeper to Her Majesty the Queen at Windsor Park, owned several splendid Deerhounds, bred from Prince Albert's Hector of Monzie's breed, and a bitch of a strain he had brought from Chillingham. At his death the writer purchased three, amongst them the well-known and superb dog Keildar and his sister Hag, a bitch of great size and very good shape, but wanting in coat.

12

Now to touch on breeders of the present day.

The Duke of Sutherland owns good-looking and useful dogs, but they are small, and a doubt is expressed in some quarters as to their *true* breeding. Regarding some of those *formerly* in his possession there, however, can be no doubt.

Mr. Spencer Lucy of Charlcote has some of the strain of Menzies of Chesthill, as before-mentioned, and has been crossing with one or two well-known prize-takers—it is believed with satisfactory results.

Mr. Gillespie of Tulloch, Kingussie, should be mentioned here, being the breeder and owner of the far-famed Torrom. Though Mr. Gillespie was hardly to be considered a breeder of Deerhounds, yet this dog was such a notoriously good one that, in justice to the subject, notice of his breeder cannot be omitted.

Mr. Donald Cameron of Lochiel is well known to Deerhound lovers as the breeder of Pirate and the giant Torrom. These dogs were from a bitch, Loy, by Mr. Gillespie's Torrom, by Campbell of Monzie's Grumach.

Mr. H. Chaworth Musters is known widely as the owner of the above-mentioned Torrom, which was purchased from "Lochiel" by a Mr. Bowles when exhibited at the Birmingham show in 1869, he then being three years old. He was afterwards purchased by Mr. Musters, and has been extensively bred from, with varied success.

Mr. R. Hood Wright has also bred some very fair Deerhounds. He is mentioned before as having the strain of Menzies of Chesthill in his kennels.

The late Sydney Dobell owned a very capital breed of Deerhound, descended from a bitch presented to him by Flora Macdonald of Skye. These dogs have had much to do with some of the best dogs now extant. They were said to be of pure Glengarry breed.

The last, and perhaps the most successful, breeder to whom allusion will be made is Mr. Thomas Morse. The dogs bred by this gentleman have proved themselves most successful candidates for public favour, and have gone to the top of the tree so far as prize-taking is concerned, and no doubt, where opportunity has offered, have proved themselves as good and true as they unquestionably are good-looking. Amongst them, Mr. Hemming's Linda, Mr. Chinnery's Duke, and Mr. Hay's Rufus, may be mentioned. Mr. Morse decidedly owes much, if not all, of his success to his judicious use of that magnificent dog Keildar, and the produce have in many instances thrown to him in a marked manner, even so far as two generations off.

Before concluding this notice of breeders, the Hon. Mrs. Deane Morgan, living in Co. Wexford, Ireland, should be mentioned, who now has dogs descended from pure strains brought from Scotland many years ago. It is believed these are fine animals, of which their owner is remarkably proud. One was given by her to Mr. George Dennis, Her Majesty's Consul in Sicily, and is reported by him to be an extraordinarily fine and noble animal. Mr. Dennis has lately taken a very well-descended young bitch out to Sicily to mate with him.

Mr. George Cupples has also bred many good dogs, amongst them Spey, now the property of Mr. Morse—selected to illustrate this article. There are several other breeders of years gone by whom the writer had perhaps better mention by name, and though he personally knows but little of their strains, they were reckoned to be remarkably good ones—namely, Lord Seaforth, McDonald of Keppoch, McKenzie of Kintail, and General Ross of Glenmoidart.

It is now proposed to allude to a few of the largest "noted" dogs—before proceeding to describe generally the "cracks" of the breed—that have arisen during the last thirty-five years.

13

Sir St. George Gore's Gruim has already been noticed. He was said to stand 32 to 33 inches (?), and was a very well-shaped and excellent dog. He was at his prime about 1843-44.

Black Bran, a 31-inch dog, in reality a black brindle, was a remarkably good dog about 1850-51.

The Marquis of Breadalbane's King of the Forest was a dog of extraordinary size, being, it is supposed, 33 inches high. He was held to be a good dog.

An unusually fine dog, called Alder, was shown many times about 1863-67—the property of Mr. Beasley, bred, it was asserted, by Sir John McNiel of Colonsay—that stood about 31½ inches, and probably weighed 110 lbs. This was a very well-shaped dog, not too bulky, of a dark brindle colour; coat very hard. Unfortunately, this dog never got any descendants worthy of himself. He was a grand animal.

In later years we have Torrom, first shown at Birmingham by his breeder, Mr. Donald Cameron of Lochiel, in 1869, he then being three years old. He afterwards passed into the possession of Mr. H. Chaworth Musters, and won numerous prizes, being known as Champion Old Torrom. This dog, as far as could be ascertained, threw back to some ancestor of gigantic size—probably Lord Breadalbane's King of the Forest. He was an extraordinarily heavy dog for a Deerhound, and usually considered lumbersome, and found too much so for work by his owner, who got rid of him for this reason. His head was very massive, and his coat very full and soft; legs by no means straight—a weakness which many of his descendants have inherited. He was a medium brownish colour, faintly brindle, very long in make; ears very coarse, and tail of extreme length. He stood 31 inches, girthed 35, and weighed, *fat*, about 110 lbs.

His two sons — Monzie, out of Brenda, bred by and the property of Mr. Musters, and Young Torrom, out of Braie, bred by Mr. Hancock—are both dogs of great size, standing 31 inches and weighing about 105 lbs.; the former considerably the better dog of the two. The latter dog was exported to America some three years ago.

Of a different strain—going direct back to McNiel's dogs—we have Hector, the property of Mr. Dadley, head-keeper to the Marquis of Bristol—a splendid dog, of darkish brindle colour, good rough coat, and well-shaped, by Giaour, out of Hylda; height, 31 inches; girth, 35; weight, 105 lbs. A good dog with deer, and thoroughly well-bred— probably the best-bred dog now extant.

His two sons—Oscar, the property of Mr. Phillips, Croxton House, Boxford, a very fine symmetrical dog, of great length, rather pale-fawn brindle, out of Lufra, a bitch of small size and somewhat uncertain pedigree, standing 31 inches and weighing about 105 lbs.; and Sir Bors, the property of Lieutenant-Colonel Leyland, a dog of similar colour, out of Lufra also (a prior litter), a very grand dog in every way. He stands 31 inches, girths 35, and weighs 105 lbs.

To go on to a general notice of the cracks. First to be noticed is Mr. Gillespie's celebrated dog Torrom, which is here described in Mr. Gillespie's own words :—"He did not stand very high, but was remarkably well formed for strength and speed; his weight I do not know; colour steel-grey (what we call blue); coat long and silky, with an undergrowth of close downy hair of a darker shade; ears small, and darker in colour than body, with silver-grey dots and tipped with silver-grey silky hair; he also had a great deal of the same silver-grey silky hair on his face; tail long and straight, with half turned to one side when erect; legs very strong, but clean and beautifully formed; feet small, round, and cat-like; chest very deep and round; neck long, arched, and strong; head small, but with wonderful power of jaw (I have seen him break the shoulder of very many red deer stags with a single twist); back very strong and arched; loins of wonderful strength. Torrom was by Faust, a dog (I believe *the last*) that belonged to Mrs. McDonnell, wife of the late Glengarry, and was one of the finest-looking dogs I have seen; his dam was Garry, a bitch given to me by Gordon Cumming when he last started for Africa. On Cumming's return I gave him back the bitch, which I believe he afterwards sold to Sir St. George Gore. Torrom when little more than a year old proved himself the best dog at deer I ever saw or expect to see.

All dogs of any note at the present time can trace their descent back to this exceedingly grand specimen of the race. Mr. Campbell of Monzie's Greumah was a particularly nice dog, got by a fine dog belonging to General Ross of Glenmoidart, of the Keppoch strain, out of a Monzie bitch. He was the sire of Pirate and Torrom, bred by Mr. Cameron of Lochiel. Mr. Cameron writes thus regarding this fine dog:—"He was a magnificent dog, not so massive as his son (Champion Torrom), but more like a Deerhound. He was a strong-framed dog, with plenty of hair, of a blue-brindle colour. He was very like the dog you refer to as belonging to Mr. Gillespie."

Keildar, bred by the late Mr. Cole, head-keeper of Windsor Park, was one of the most elegant and aristocratic-looking Deerhounds ever seen. He was a dog of great length, and yet possessed great speed and power. He was in constant use in Windsor Park for stalking deer, and was very adept at his work. He showed high breeding and symmetry to a remarkable extent. His height was a full 30 inches, girth 33½, and weight 95 lbs.; colour bluish-fawn, slightly brindled, the muzzle and ears being blue; coat rather soft in character and tolerably full. He was by a handsome dog (Oscar), belonging to Mr. Bridge, of the breed of McKenzie of Applecross. His descendants have made their mark by their size, high breeding, and good looks. Amongst them are the well-known Linda, which resembles her sire in an extraordinary degree, his son Rufus, and amongst his grandsons Hector and Duke, Mr. Phillips' Oscar and Lieut.-Colonel Leyland's Sir Bors being his great-grandsons. Mr. Field's Bran, own brother, same litter as Keildar, was only slightly his inferior, and in most ways a very similar dog. Amongst his descendants Morni is perhaps the most remarkable. Mr. Cyril Dobell—brother to Sydney—owned a capital dog of good size in Bevis, the sire of Linda's dam and other good dogs. He was a sandy dog of good coat, stood 30 inches, and weighed probably near 100 lbs., being rather short in make. Major Robertson's Oscar, a nice brindle dog of good coat, long made, bred by General Ross of Glenmoidart, stood about 29 inches, and was a well-made, handsome dog. From him were bred some good dogs out of Sydney Dobell's Maida, and he was the sire of Morni out of a bitch by Field's Bran, out of Carrac.

Mr. Hickman's Morni was a nice dog, of a greyish-brindle colour, coat somewhat soft. He stood 30 inches, girthed 34, and weighed about 98 lbs. Showed quality and breeding.

Pirate, the property of Cameron of Lochiel, and own brother to the celebrated Champion Old Torrom (Mr. Musters'), was a smaller, more compact, and far better-made dog than his gigantic brother. Very dark in colour—blue-brindle—he had a harder and more dense coat than Torrom, and was in every respect his superior. He stood about 29 inches, and was considered "perfect" at work by his owner. He got some very nice stock, but none, it is believed, proved large, though capital dogs for work.

Duke, at one time the property of Mr. Chinnery, winner of several first prizes, was a dark, grizzled, hard-coated dog—perhaps somewhat deficient in hair on head and legs—and a

15

handsome, well-built dog, though somewhat light of bone. He stood 30 inches, and was a fairly lengthy dog.

Spey, the bitch selected for illustration, was bred by Mr. Cupples, and has been owned for many years by Mr. Morse, who has bred many very superior dogs from her. She is about 27 inches in height and of a lengthy frame. Coat very hard and good. Colour is shown in illustration. Duke was her son, and resembled her strongly in coat and colour. She is a well-descended bitch, of thoroughly good appearance.

Mr. Musters' Young Torrom, winner of an extraordinary number of prizes, is a much superior dog to his sire, Old Champion Torrom, but is considerably his inferior in size. He is a dark slate colour, with a lighter head, of not very taking expression, extremely long and strong in make ; coat soft and dense. A striking feature in this strain is their very long sweeping tail. His height is about 29½ inches.

Mr. Wright's Bevis, a darkish red-brown brindle dog of about 29 inches, is a thoroughly well-bred dog ; perhaps, excepting Hector, the best bred Deerhound out. His coat is very long and shaggy, and extends itself to his ears, very much to the detriment of his appearance. · He is a compact, well-shaped dog.

Dr. Haddon has shown a handsome bitch, called Lufra, with a remarkably handsome head and good coat—which former feature she has transmitted to her son, by Young Torrom (Mr. Musters'), Roy by name. The bitch has no ascertained pedigree.

There are many other good and fine dogs scattered through the country which could be mentioned ; but as this is not a stud book, it is considered unnecessary to do so.

The Deerhound will now be closely described. As regards size many arguments are put forward. In former days when the red deer was coursed (as hares are) without having previously been wounded, the larger and more powerful the dog was, provided that the Greyhound's speed and activity were preserved, the more was he valued ; but in these degenerate days, when deer are usually brought to book without the aid of dogs or often even in their presence, an *animal* that can find and bay a wounded stag is considered to be all that is required. In some few cases the Deerhound proper is used, but this is being fast allowed to fall into disuse in the majority of cases. To run into and hold a full-grown stag, a large and strong dog is certainly required, and it was found that a dog averaging 29 to 30 inches was the correct animal. His girth should be great and chest deep—without being too flat-sided ; for a 30-inch dog, 34 inches should be the average. The fore-arm, below elbow, should measure 8½ inches, and the dog weigh from 95 to 105 lbs. Should the dog stand as much as 31 inches, as is sometimes the case, these dimensions would be slightly exceeded. He should be of lengthy make. The average for bitches, which are very much less than the dogs, would be as follows :— Height, 26 inches ; girth, 29 inches ; weight, 65 to 70 lbs. In figure and conformation this dog should closely approximate to the smooth Greyhound, allowance being made for his superior stature and bulk. The head should be long and lean, rather wider behind the ears, yet not suddenly widening ; neck long, strong, and arched ; body long ; back slightly curved upwards, descending towards tail ; legs very strong and straight ; feet round, well and firmly set ; quarters well-developed, and equal to propelling the animal with extreme velocity ; ears small, semi-erect, dark in colour, and smooth, though several strains—really good ones — show a hairy ear ; tail long and free from curl, having a curve towards the tip only. The general appearance should be striking, elegant, and aristocratic to a marked extent, and nobility of carriage is a very strong feature in the breed. The coat should be coarse and hard, full and dense on head, body, legs, and tail, without being "exaggerated;" that on the head should be softer in character than that on the body ; the hair over eyes and under jaws being of greater length, and rather more wiry than that on the rest of the head. The well-covered head gives much "character," and adds vastly to the general beauty of this magnificent dog. The length of the hair should be from three to four inches. Some breeders hold that no Deerhound is worthy of notice unless he has a good rough head, with plenty of beard and coat generally.; also, that the purity of a smooth skulled dog is to be doubted. Here, however, they are at fault, as several of the best known dogs have had nearly smooth heads.

In colour the Deerhound varies much—from *nearly* black, through dark brindle, blue, light brindle, grey, fawn, and sandy, and cream of all shades, to pure white. Black-and-tan dogs of the breed have also been known. As a matter of taste, the darker colours, as iron-grey and brindle, are to be preferred; but many first-class specimens have been and are of a lighter colour. On a dark. heath a light-coloured dog shows plainer.

These dogs are usually remarkably fine and graceful jumpers, and possessed of great activity. In the matter of speed they often equal the smooth Greyhound, but owing to their great size are unequal to making such quick turns as their smaller congener. The scenting powers are developed in a remarkable way, and many wonderful tales are told of the tracking powers of these dogs. When unsighted, they often recover for their masters "cold" stags by their unerring powers in this line.

They are bad swimmers, but occasionally will take the water, and never shrink from it when in pursuit of their quarry.

The Deerhound is justly considered a difficult dog to rear, and to a certain degree delicate, though some authors put him forward as being the "hardiest of the hardy." They also are not a long-lived dog.

It was supposed that the gradual dying out of the practice of coursing the red deer would soon put an end to the breeding of the Deerhound ; but such, happily, is not the case. This dog, in reality, has wonderfully increased the last twenty years, and is now, compara-tively speaking, common. His beauty, gentleness, power, and courage, have so recommended him as a pet and companion, and his appearance is so ornamental and graceful, that he is highly esteemed by all the gentle in the land ; and the fear that the breed would become extinct has long since vanished.

The late Sir St. George Gore, a breeder of experience, was of opinion that the Deer-hounds of the present day are far finer than they were thirty and forty years ago ; also that a dog could not then be found to run at 85 lbs., whereas now the standard is from 90 to 100 lbs.

Since Lord Henry Bentinck's demise in 1871 no *large* kennels of Deerhounds remain. Formerly there were from twenty to sixty kept in several kennels ; at the same time, many magnificent specimens *are* scattered broadcast through the land, as many as six or seven, or even more, being in the same hands, and it is probable that instead of having decreased in numbers it has increased considerably; where *one* person owned a Deerhound or two formerly twenty do so now. Lord Breadalbane, the Duke of Athol, Lord H. Bentinck, "Glengarry," and others, kept large kennels of these superb dogs, but they have all passed away now.

This article will hardly be considered complete unless some allusion be made to the much-vexed question of cross-breeding.

17

"Idstone" says :—" Many crosses have been adopted, as I have already observed, and one of the Deerhound and Mastiff has been used by the proprietor of a deer-pack in my immediate neighbourhood, where there is a fine herd of red and fallow deer. Though I prefer the Deerhound, it must be granted that whilst the breed was not procurable such a measure as manufacturing a dog for the work was meritorious. The best I have noticed of this description were produced by the skill and patience of Mr. Norwood, of the South-Western Railway, at Waterloo. I have never seen these hounds in action, but I have been assured that nothing can be finer than their work. They had the race-horse points, the long neck, the clean head, the bright intellectual eye, the long sloping shoulder, the muscular arms, the straight legs, the close well-knit feet, the wide muscular arched back and loins, the deep back ribs, the large girth, the *esprit*, the life, the activity which when controlled and schooled is essential to every domesticated animal."

It is a well-known fact that the late "Glengarry," finding the breed of Deerhound deteriorating, resorted to several crosses—amongst them the Cuban Bloodhound and Pyrenean Wolfdog ; from the latter especially he gained much. He was at the time condemned loudly for thus contaminating the breed ; but, in the writer's opinion, he acted with great good judgment, for he resuscitated his strain very completely, and from his so-crossed dogs have all our modern Deerhounds descended, all symptoms of any such cross having long been obliterated. Mr. Gillespie, the owner and breeder of *the* notorious Torrom, says :—" With regard to your remark about the Glengarry dogs not being pure, I too have often heard it ; but my *experience* is that there were few, if any, better strains." His Torrom was the son of a true Glengarry dog. Of this breed also was the world-wide-famed Maida, Sir Walter Scott's devoted and constant companion ; but he was the offspring of the first cross between Pyrenean Wolfdog and Highland Deerhound, the former being sire, the latter dam. He was a magnificent animal, of great size, power, and endurance, partaking mostly of the appearance of the dam, gaining somewhat in power, bulk, and height from the sire. He was of an iron-grey colour (according to Irving), and of gigantic size. He died at eleven years of age. From this very Maida many of our best modern dogs claim descent!

A gentleman who has had much experience in breeding Deerhounds for the last thirty years and upwards, and who has bred many grand dogs, says :—" My brother informs me that McNiel *went all over the world* to get dogs to breed from—to Albania amongst other places—and that his breed represents a breed he himself founded, and that prior to that there was no real existing breed of Deerhounds in Scotland (! !). I think that their extreme delicacy and the difficulty of rearing them, also the way in which they feel the cold in bad weather in October, indicate their foreign origin."

It is thought that there must have been some misapprehension on this matter, as, putting aside the existence of Morison of Scalascraig's breed in 1830 (McNiel's dating a few years later), as well as that of Menzies of Chesthill, asserted to date from 1780 or thereabouts, Lord Colonsay, then Sir J. McNiel, communicated with the writer about 1865 in the following terms :—" There seems to be no doubt that the Deerhound of the Celtic Highlands is of precisely the same race as the Irish hound sometimes called Wolfhound ; and all attempts to get size or speed by crossing have, it is believed, failed, or only succeeded in giving size by destroying the characteristics of the race. I imported Wolfhounds from Russia of fair speed and large size, but silky-haired, with a view to cross them with the Deerhound, but the result was by no means satisfactory. The late Lord Breadalbane crossed with the Bloodhound, and produced some good Retrievers for his deer-stalking ; but they were no

18

longer Deerhounds. The Macedonian Dog—a very powerful, smooth dog—was also imported by a member of my family without any better results; and it is my conviction that the race of Deerhounds can be improved only by careful selection and crossing different strains of pure blood."

The above remarks were shown to a friend of the writer who had given a full trial to crossing for size, &c. He says :—"I do not agree with Sir J. McNiel in all he says I think with you that he did not continue his experiments far enough. Then, again, speed was the element he aimed at chiefly, and it is not to be expected he would retain that when crossing with a slower dog."

The writer has not the smallest doubt—looking at the grand dogs we now possess—that the various crosses tried have in most instances profited very much the breed, which had evidently fallen into a degenerate state forty to fifty years ago. He knows by experience that all trace of a cross disappears as a rule in the second or third generation, and the dog has *in every way* the appearance and characteristics of a Deerhound proper. The cross from Russian Wolfhound, judiciously used, has certainly imparted to the Deerhound a degree of quality and certain blood-like look that the breed was fast losing, to say nothing of the gain in the matter of symmetry that almost invariably accrues.

It is a most noticeable and curious fact that the purer the breed is the more marked is the disparity between the sexes in the Deerhound. Thus, if two *pure* bred dogs be used, the difference between the sexes will vary from four to six inches in height; whereas, if the female parent be cross-bred and of large size, the difference between the males and females of the litter will only be two inches, and, oddly enough, even if the bitch so bred shall vastly exceed the truer bred one in size, the dog puppies from her—by an equally fine dog—will generally in no way exceed in size those from the smaller but truer bred bitch.

That size can more surely be obtained through the sire than through the dam is a fact worth remembering.

It is much to be regretted that the pedigrees of the prominent specimens of this breed have not been retained, but there is little doubt but that most of our existing cracks can claim them as their progenitors. In future there will be no trouble on this head, as the very admirable stud-books established about 1870 will obviate this.

Before concluding this article, the writer would strongly impress on all readers the extreme desirability of retaining, by judicious care and cultivation, this, of all dogs (save his undoubted progenitor the Irish Wolfhound), the most beautiful and picturesque, as well as the most majestic and ornamental—an animal to be loved and valued, and treated as a friend, as he richly deserves to be in all but rare cases.

The accompanying engraving, which so faithfully represents some Deerhounds on the watch, is the work of the great German artist, Specht. Though the dogs do not quite come up to modern ideas of show form in every minute particular, the artistic arrangement of the group is to the life, and thoroughly conveys in all essential respects the character of the dog, and what a Deerhound should be.

The dog selected for the coloured plate is Mr. Morse's Spey, who may be taken as one of the best specimens of the breed in existence, though not shown. She was nearly twelve years old in January, 1880, when she scaled 73 lbs., and measured as follows :—From tip of nose to stop, 4½ inches ; length from stop to occipital bone, 5¾ inches ; girth of skull behind the eyes, 15 inches ; girth of neck, 15 inches ; girth round shoulders, 30 inches ; girth of loins, 20¾ inches ;

19

SCOTCH DEERHOUNDS.

20

girth of thigh, 16½ inches; girth of forearm, 7 inches; height at shoulders, 26 inches; height at elbows, 14½ inches; height at loins, 26 inches; height at hock, 7½ inches; length of tail, 22 inches. The above must be considered exceptionally good measurements when the advanced age of the dog comes to be considered.

An extremely good bitch, too, which came before the public in 1879, is Heather, the property of the Rev. Grenville F. Hodson, of North Petherton, Bridgwater, which gentleman is one of our oldest Deerhound breeders, and a recognised judge of the variety. Mr. Graham has, we believe, not seen Heather, and has therefore omitted her from the list he gives above.

As in the case of the Irish Wolfhound, Mr. Graham in his article did not append a scale of points. We therefore give the following on our own responsibility.

SCALE OF POINTS FOR JUDGING DEERHOUNDS.

								Value.
Skull	...	...	...	...	...	...	...	10
Neck	...	...	...	...	...	...	...	5
Body	...	...	...	...	...	...	...	10
Legs and feet	...	...	...	...	...	...	...	10
Coat	...	...	...	...	...	...	...	10
General appearance		...	...	...	...	...	...	5
				Total	...	...	...	50

THE DEERHOUND.

FAILING any further information on the subject than we at present possess, it will always be a moot point whether the hounds used for Queen Elizabeth's delectation at Cowdray Park, in 1595, that "pulled down sixteen bucks in a laund," were ordinary greyhounds or Scottish deerhounds. The latter were likely enough to be fashionable animals at the close of the sixteenth century, for they had already been described by Hector Boece, in his History of Scotland, printed in France 1526-7, which by royal command was translated into English in 1531. Thirty years later, Gesner, in his " General History of Quadrupeds," gives an illustration of three " Scottish dogs," one of them answering to our modern deerhound in general appearance. The drawing for this was supplied by Henry St. Clair, Dean of Glasgow at that time, whose family kept the breed for very many years, an interesting story in connection therewith being told on another page.

Good Queen Bess was fond of her dogs and the sport they showed, and there is nothing unreasonable in supposing that those provided for the purpose above-mentioned in Cowdray Park were in reality deerhounds. However, whether my supposition be correct or otherwise, there is no gainsaying the fact that this mention in the Scottish history is the earliest to be met with where the deerhound is actually alluded to.

That he was highly valued by the clans or chieftains of his native country may be judged from the following pretty story told by Boece. On one occasion many of the Pictish nobility repaired to Craithlint, to meet the King of Scots to hunt and make merry with him, where they found the Scottish dogs far excelled their own in "fairness, swiftness, and hardness, and also in long standing up and holding out." The Scottish lords gave their guests both dogs and bitches of their best strains; but they, not contented, stole one, belonging to the king, from his keeper; and this the most esteemed hound in the lot. The master of the leash being informed of the robbery, pursuit was taken after the thievish Picts, who, being overtaken, refused to give up the royal favourite, and in the end slew the master of the leash with their spears. Then the Scots mustered a stronger force, including those who had been engaged in hunting, and they fell upon the Picts. A terrible struggle took place, one hundred of the Picts were slain and "threescore gentlemen" on the other side, besides a great number of commoners. The latter, poor fellows, not being deemed worthy of numeration in those bloodthirsty times, and, so long as the hound was recovered, little thought would be given to the dead "commoners" who fought for its possession. Moreover, it was stated few of the combatants knew what they had been fighting about.

Another interesting story is that relating to the family of St. Clair. King Robert Bruce, in following the chase upon the Pentland Hills, had often started a "white faunch deer," which always escaped from his hounds. He asked his nobles if any of them possessed dogs that they thought might prove more successful. Naturally, there was no one there so bold as to affirm his hounds better than those of the sovereign, until Sir William St. Clair came forward. He would wager his head that his two favourite hounds, "Help" and "Hold," would kill the deer before she could cross the March burn. Bruce, evidently of a sporting turn, at once wagered the Forest of Pentland Moor, to the head of the bold Sir William, against the accomplishment of the feat. The deer was roused by the slow, or drag hounds, and St. Clair, in a suitable place, uncoupled his favourites in sight of the flying hind. St. Clair followed on horseback, and as the deer reached the middle of the brook, he in despair, believing his wager already lost, and his life as good as gone, leaped from his horse. At this critical moment, " Hold " stopped her quarry in the brook, and " Help " coming up, the deer was turned, and in the end killed within the stipulated boundary. The king, not far behind, was soon on the scene, and, embracing his subject, " bestowed on him the lands of Kirton, Logan House, Earncraig, &c., in free forestrie." Scrope says the tomb of this Sir William St. Clair, on which he appears sculptured in armour, with a greyhound (deerhound) at his feet, is still to be seen in Rosslyn Chapel.

A common but erroneous idea has prevailed, that the Irish wolfhound and the Scottish deerhound were identical, and, indeed, that the latter was merely an ordinary greyhound, with a rough, hard coat, produced by beneficent Nature to protect a delicate dog against the rigours of a northern climate.

About the end of the sixteenth century (1591), we are told that the Earl of Mar had large numbers of deerhounds, but at the same period the Duke of Buckingham had great difficulty in obtaining Irish wolf dogs, a few couples of which he wished to present to "divers princes and other nobles." So the Irish dog was even then becoming extinct, but the Scottish one survives to the present day, and is now more popular and numerous than at any previous period of his existence. Still, judging from what Pennant, writing in 1769, says, the deerhound must, about his time, have been rare in certain districts, for he says, " he saw at Gordon Castle a true Highland greyhound, which has become very scarce. It was of large size, strong, deep chested, and covered with very long and rough hair. This kind was in great vogue in former days, and used in vast numbers at the magnificent stag chases by powerful chieftains." Even the Kings of Scotland were wont to command those of their subjects who had good hounds to bring them together in order that they should have a suitable hunt, and their commands were freely responded to by the presence of the Earls of Argyle, Huntly, Athol, and others.

Towards the close of the past century and early in the present one the deerhound was by no means so uncommon in various parts of Scotland as some have inferred. A good many were scattered up and down in various holdings, especially in the western portions of the Highlands, extending to the Hebrides. The smaller farmers kept one or two, and so did many of the shepherds, who were never loth to chase and kill a deer, and when a stag, or even hind, was not to be had, the deerhound was trained to hunt and kill foxes and otters, and other small game or vermin. After the rebellion of 1745, a good deal of uneasiness and unpleasantness remained, and the animosity caused thereby was a long time in being allayed. In many instances the Highland residences were neglected, their owners going to reside on the Continent or elsewhere. Their hounds were, therefore, spread abroad in out-of-the-way places, and thus perhaps came the impression conveyed by Pennant of their scarcity. Mr. George Cupples ("Scotch Deerhounds and their Masters") tells us the lowlier families used these hounds in competing against each other, and matches between certain celebrated hounds in adjoining districts were frequent. No doubt the deerhound, under such surroundings, would improve, especially as he was, to a certain extent, more of a companion than when kept in a large kennel.

In Johnson's tour to the Hebrides in 1773, Boswell makes several allusions to the dogs and hounds. He says : " In the Isle of Sky is a race of brindled greyhounds larger and stronger than those with which we course hares, and these are the only dogs used by them (the islanders) for the chase. . . . . The deer are not driven with horns and hounds.

A sportsman with a gun in his hand watches the animal, and when he has wounded him traces him by the blood." The same quaint volume says that on one occasion the young laird of Coll "was sporting in the mountains of Sky, and when weary with following his game repaired to Talisker. At night he missed one of his dogs, and when he went to seek for him in the morning found two eagles feeding on his carcase." Scottish hounds were by no means uncommon then in the Hebrides and on the western coast, where considerable pains were taken to preserve the strain in its purity and strength, and no doubt, in a great measure, we are indebted to these smaller farmers for preserving a fine variety of the canine race when it was within quite an easy distance of almost entire extinction. It is possible that, had the Irish wolfhound been favoured in a similar manner, and obtained equally warm admirers, there would have been no occasion for the resuscitation of the breed by the introduction of the deerhound and German boarhound cross.

One or two authors have assumed that the modern deerhound is a cross between the foxhound and the greyhound, or between the bloodhound and the greyhound, but this I consider quite incorrect, nor in my researches have I been able to come across anything likely to sustain such a statement. If the deerhound is to be found in greater numbers now than previously, it is only because more attention is paid to his breeding, and because the many strains that a hundred years and more ago were in the out of the way places of the Highlands have, by better communication, been brought within the radius of canine admirers. Scrope, in his "Deer Stalking," published in 1838, has naturally much to write about the deerhound. He it is recommends the foxhound and greyhound cross, and says that the celebrated sportsman Glengarry crossed occasionally with bloodhounds, still Macneill of Colonsay, who wrote the article in "Days of Deerstalking," that deals mostly with those hounds, confesses that there were still pure deerhounds to be found when he states them to be very scarce at the time he wrote. Maybe they were scarce, but not sufficiently so as to induce people to attempt to reproduce them by such an unhallowed alliance, and perhaps, as stated above, they were not quite so scarce as he imagined. In addition to the hounds kept by the farmers and shepherds, Lord Seaforth had a large kennel, and the strains of the MacDonnels of Invergary House, of Cluny Macpherson, of Colonel Mitchell Strathmaspie, of the Lochiels in Lochaber, one of whose hounds was said to have killed the last wolf in Scotland ; of the Dukes of Gordon, of the

McKenzies, Macraes, and Macleods, were all of considerable reputation. The pedigrees were carefully guarded, and it is said that Dr. Ross, parish priest at Kilmonivaig, was prouder of the blood of some of his hounds, which were said to be of a pure and rare strain originally possessed by the Duke of Gordon, than he was of his own ancestry, traceable to the Earls of Ross.

A favourite sporting author from my earliest boyhood days has been Charles St. John, who, in his "Highland Sports," writes so charmingly and naturally of all he saw and shot and caught during his excursions. He wrote but eight years after Scrope, still he says that the breed of deerhounds which "had nearly become extinct, or, at any rate, was very rare a few years ago, has now become comparatively plentiful in all the Highland districts, owing to the increased extent of the preserved forests and the trouble taken by different proprietors and masters of mountain shootings, who have collected and bred this noble race of dogs regardless of expense and difficulty." Not a word about Macneill's crosses or of those of Glengarry; and I am happy in the belief that our present race of deerhounds does not contain the slightest taint of bloodhound or foxhound blood. If it did, surely the black and tan colour and the greyhound markings would continually be appearing.

I have yet to see a black and tan deerhound, or one similar to a foxhound in hue.

What a striking and life-like picture St. John draws of Malcolm : "as fine a looking lad, of thirty-five, as ever stepped on heather," and of his two hounds, Bran and Oscar, whose descriptions tally with what I shall later on give to be those of a deerhound. There was no bloodhound or foxhound stain in Bran and Oscar, and well might such handsome, useful, faithful creatures, or similar ones, be worth the £50 a-piece they would have brought even forty-five years ago.

Since St. John wrote, many deer forests have been broken up into smaller holdings, and to this, perhaps, may be attributed the fact that "coursing deer" is not followed so much as in his time. There are still a few forests in which a deerhound may be taken out to assist at the termination of a stalk ; but as the red deer is now mostly killed in "drives," a sort of battue in which the shooter can sit at ease until the deer come along, to be shot in a somewhat ignominious manner, the deerhound as such is little used. A stalker will find one useful at times, but even he is supplied with such a perfect rifle, so admirably sighted, and he is such a good shot that the stag seldom requires more than the hard bullet to kill him almost dead upon the spot.

Some few years ago the Earl of Tankerville, in a series of articles he wrote for the *Field*, made allusion to the deerhound. He said many that he saw " were beautiful, swift, and powerful. Some are able to pull down a stag single handed, but the bravest always gets killed in the end. The pure breed have keen noses as well as speed, and will follow the slot of a wounded deer perseveringly if they find blood. The most valued are not necessarily the most savage, for the latter (the reckless ones) go in and get killed, whilst the more wary, who have taken the hint after a pug or two, are equally enduring, and will hold their bay for any indefinite time, which is a merit of the first importance."

Lord Tankerville continues, that he was informed of a remarkable deerhound, belonging to a poacher in Badenoch, that never missed a deer. In due course he obtained the hound, and called it Bran. Later on it saved the life of a keeper from the furious attack of one of the wild bulls of Chillingham. After being delivered to his new home, Bran was placed in the kennel, and it was thought that the pallisades with which it was surrounded were sufficiently high to prevent any dog getting over them. However, Bran did succeed in scaling them, and Lord Tankerville, having paid his money and lost his dog, was considerably upset, and never thought of seeing the hound again. However, in a few days the "poacher" brought back the errant Bran, who had, in fact, reached his old home before his master, who was considerably astonished, on reaching his cottage, to see his old companion rush forward to meet him. The distance between Chillingham and the man's cottage was about seventy miles, and to take the shortest route, which Bran no doubt did or he would have caught his master on the road, he must have swum Loch Ericht.

Naturally modern dog shows have done much to re-popularise the deerhound, now that he is so seldom required for that purpose for which, shall I say, nature first intended him. How little he is used in deer stalking may be surmised by a list that appears in Mr. Weston Bell's monograph of the variety (1892). Here some fifty-eight forests are named, and in but about seven of them is the deerhound kept. The collie is now more frequently trained and used to track the wounded stag, because he works more slowly, and is therefore less liable to unduly scare and alarm the deer. From the earliest institution of dog shows, classes have been provided for the deerhound, and these have resulted in a number of excellent animals being benched of a uniformity and quality that our excellent friend Charles St. John would scarcely have thought possible, and Archibald Macneill would have deemed incomprehensible.

There is no handsomer dog than the deerhound—he has the elegance of shape, the light, airy appearance of the greyhound, a hard, crisp, and picturesque jacket, either of fawn or grey brindle, an eye as bright as that of the gazelle, but loving, still sharp and intelligent; and a good specimen has not a bad feature about him. His disposition is of the best; he is sensible and kindly; and friends of mine to whom I gave a puppy, on its death refused to be consoled by any other dog than one of the same variety.

"It's a blooming lurcher," is the yokel's idea of a deerhound, an opinion in which the cockney corner man evidently coincides. Either will pass a rude remark about your aristocratic canine companion. The Scotsman away from home, be he out at elbows, or otherwise, pays compliments to the dog. If his shoes are down at the heels, the chances are he is the sole survival of a chieftain of some great clan, and, on the strength of your possession of one of his native quadrupeds, will seek to allay his thirst, or penchant for Glenlivat, at your expense. Still, I do not fancy that the deerhound is quite so popular as a companion over the border as he is on this side the border. Englishmen have paid greater attention to his breeding; the honours to be gained at shows make it worth while their doing so; and, being more difficult to rear than most other dogs, he requires greater care in bringing up, and, if not allowed continual exercise, will become crooked on his fore legs, and out at the elbows—ungainly enough in little dogs, but a terrible eyesore in big ones. They will not rear well in a kennel.

It has been said the deerhound is uncertain in his temper with children; in some cases this may be so, but not in all. Again, it has been stated that when a puppy he will chase anything that moves in front of him—sheep, poultry, &c. What puppy will not? All young dogs are alike in this particular, and if not carefully watched will, like your favourite little boy or girl, be for ever getting into mischief.

Deerhounds, like all dogs, require careful early training, and when once broken off sheep and other "small deer," are as safe and reliable in the fields as any other of the canine race. As a fact, I believe that both pointers and setters, greyhounds, and even the collie himself, is as "fond of mutton" as the often maligned dog about which this article is being written. Many dogs have been spoiled by their manners being neglected during their puppyhood; no doubt others will be so in the future, and it is a pity that one so docile, handsome, sagacious, and aristocratic as the deerhound, should obtain an evil name through the negligence or over-indulgence of its owner.

As already stated, dog shows have been of infinite advantage in raising the deerhound to its present popularity, though prior to this epoch, what Sir Walter Scott writes of his Maida and other favourite hounds, with Landseer's fine paintings, had made the general public anxious to see such handsome hounds in the flesh. The first show at Birmingham, in 1860, provided two classes for them, but there were few entries, and both leading prizes were taken by Lieut.-Colonel Inge, of Thorpe, near Tamworth, who, at that time, possessed a capital strain of deerhounds. Later on the numbers increased, and in 1862 there were ten competitors in the dog class, but they were a mixed lot, though the winner, called Alder, bred by Sir John Macneil, was a splendid specimen, which again took leading honours two years later. The succeeding show had, for some reason or other, a capital entry, sixteen in the one class, six in the other, and these included several dogs from the Highlands, one of the latter, called Oscar, now beating Alder, who looked old and worn, and was past his best.

About this period Lord Henry Bentinck took great pride in his deerhounds, and kept a fine kennel of them. In 1870 they were sold by auction in

McDowell's rooms, Edinburgh, when sixteen hounds realised 296*l*. 16*s*. The highest figures were 50 guineas for the thirteen-year-old Factor, 40 guineas for Elshee, 30 guineas for Fury, the others bringing 30, 26, 20, and 19 guineas respectively. Mr. McKenzie, Ross-shire; Mr. J. Wright, Yeldersby House, Derby; Mr. Menzies, Chesthill; Mr. Grant, Glenmorriston; Colonel Campbell of Monzie; Mr. Wright-Omaston; Lord Boswell; Mr. W. Gordon, Guardbridge, Fifeshire; Lord Bredalbane; the Duke of Sutherland; Mr. Spencer Lucy; Mr. George Cupples, author of "Scotch Deerhounds and their Masters"; and Dr. Hadden, have at one time or another had good deerhounds in their kennels, as well as many others of the older Scottish families. The Dukes of Richmond and Gordon for generations kept a fine kennel of deerhounds, and the remnants thereof, which included a couple or two of grand old hounds, were brought from the Highlands to Aldridge's in London, where they were sold by auction in 1895, realising sorry prices, varying only from one guinea to six guineas each.

In 1869 we find a Cameron of Lochiel sending to Curzon Hall and taking a first prize with Torum, who afterwards became the property of Mr. H. C. Musters. Torum had been sent from the Highlands because he was too big for work, and Mr. Donald

Cameron was surprised at his winning, for his hound stood 32in. in height, and weighed 120lb The following year he sent Pirate and Shellock, brother and sister to Torum, and both much bettei than he in symmetry as well as in work. However, size again told, as it so often does now, and Torum won once more, with Pirate second, whilst the bitch was first in her class. Sir St. George Gore was a frequent exhibitor, and in 1865 he showed a deerhound that was almost smooth, a big coarse, ugly greyhound in appearance, that of course did not take a prize. Mr. H. C. Musters, Captain Graham, of Rednock; Mr. J. H. Beasley, Northampton; Mr. G. W. Hickman, Birmingham, and a few others who admired the fine form of the Scotch hound, were exhibiting about 1870. The following year had Mr. Dawes' Warrior, who won so many prizes up and down the country, mostly in variety classes. However, prior to him came one or two exceptionally good hounds, Mr. Beasley's bitch Countess especially so; nor must Mr. Hickman's excellent dog Morni be omitted, for he was not only good to look at, but could boast a lineage which contained some of the bluest blood of the day. Indeed, it was said by many good judges that Morni was far ahead of any deerhound they ever saw, and that, even with the accident to his stern, which necessitated his retirement after three years' successes, he was good enough to beat the best. Another almost perfect deerhound was Mr. Hickman's Lord of the Isles, of whom a Cameron of Lochiel said he was beyond criticism. The head of this splendid hound is printed on the little pamphlet issued by the Deerhound Club, and which contains its rules. Unfortunately Mr. Hickman only obtained one litter of puppies by him, but of these Fingal was sire of more good hounds of one uniform type than perhaps any other dog of the variety who has succeeded him ; to wit, Enterprise, Earl II., Ensign, Esquire, Rossie Blake, Brian, Bruar, Beppa, Blue Bonnet, and some few others.

Lord of the Isles, bred by Mr. H. P. Parkes, in 1875, was a grandson of Morni, and during his show career was pretty well invincible. Tara, a daughter of Cuchullin and Morna, all with Morni for their sire, were "lions" in their day; and Mr. Hickman subsequently owned Barra, Princess Marjorie, and many more, which were always well able to at any rate hold their own, at the Birmingham, London, Warwick, and other large shows where they were entered. Following a few years later was that fine old hound Bevis (Mr. Hood Wright's), so sober and sedate that in his declining years he took to the stage, and appeared with great success at one or two of the Sheffield pantomimes at Christmas.

There are now, at least a dozen shows held annually, at which classes are provided for this variety, and naturally new breeders have sprung up. Mr. J. Harriott Bell, of Rossie, Perthshire, has got together a' kennel containing a number of splendid deerhounds (this kennel was originally established by Mr. E. Weston Bell, whose untimely death was much regretted); and Mr. W. H. Singer, of Frome, Somerset; Mr. Walter Evans, Birchfield Birmingham; Mr. R. H. Wright, Frome; Mr. W. Gibbons, Stratford-on-Avon; Mr. A. Maxwell, now of Bedford, formerly of Croft, near Darlington; Major Davis, Bath; Miss Rattray, Swindon; the Duchess of Wellington; Mr. M. Goulter, Hungerford, Mr. W. C. Grew, Moseley, Birmingham; and Mr. H. Rawson, Midlothian, all possess deerhounds of the highest merit. Perhaps the best of their race during most recent years have been or are: Sir Gavin, Fingall II., Earl II., Ensign, Shepherd, Swift, Enterprise, Royal Lufra (a beautiful headed bitch, for which excellence she won a special prize at Bath a few years ago), Rossie Blue Bell, Rossie Blue Bonnet, Rossie Beppa, Selwood Morven, and Mr. Jenner's Dinah; the latter one of the old sort, not too big, abounding in character, and possessing a charming look out. And there are many others, almost if not equally good to look at, on the show bench.

The deerhound, in colour, should be either brindled in various shades, blue, or fawn ; white is detrimental, though a little on the chest or feet does not matter very much. Pure white dogs are occasionally found, but it is not a deerhound colour, any more than it is that of a collie, though Mr. Morton Campbell, jun., of Stracathro, near Brechin, had a white hound of considerable beauty; it was obtained from the Highlands, and its pedigree is unknown. I prefer the darker shades of colour ; the darker brindles are very attractive, and, in actual work, it is a colour that tones well with the surrounding rocks and dark heather. The largest and heaviest dogs are not to be recommended, either for work or otherwise, they cut themselves on the rocks, and are not nearly so active and lithe on the rough ground as the lighter and smaller specimens. The dog should not, at any rate, be more than about thirty inches at the shoulder, the bitch from one to two inches less. One or two specimens have been shown, and won prizes too, that measured up to thirty-two inches, and even an inch more, and it is said that Bran, figured in "Dogs of the British Isles," was thirty-three inches! At the Kennel Club's show in October, 1896, Mr. W. C. Grew showed an eighteen months puppy called Kelso which measured 32¾ inches in height. This was certainly the best big deerhound I ever saw, for there was no coarseness about him, and he was thoroughly symmetrical, although losing somewhat in character on account of his rather light coloured eyes. He won all the prizes he could win, including one given to the best deerhound in the exhibition.

The following heights and weights of some of the best deerhounds of the modern standard may be interesting, and all are excellent specimens in every way, and perhaps equal to anything that has yet been seen. Mr. Walter Evan's Fingal II. stands 29¾ inches at shoulder, and weighs 87lb.; his Earl II., 28¾ inches and 81lb.; Duke of Brewood, 30¼ inches, weighs 88lb.; and his bitch, Enterprise, stands 29 inches, and weighs 85lb., a big weight for a bitch. Mr. W. H. Singer's well-known dog, Swift, is 79lb. weight, and 30 inches at the shoulder; and his bitch, She, weighs 72lb., and stands 26½ inches.

> With eyes of sloe,
> And ears not low;
> With horse's breast,
> And deep in chest;
> And broad in loin,
> And strong in groin;
> And nape set far behind the head—
> These were the dogs that Fingal bred.

In general form the deerhound should be like a greyhound : ears similar, loins likewise, legs and feet equally good. In his character he differs from the smooth hound considerably, as he does in coat, which is hard, crisp, and close, not too long, whilst silkiness on the top knot, and elsewhere, is not desirable. In galloping or running he carries his head higher than a greyhound, nor does he lay himself down so closely to his work; he appears, indeed, to be on the look out for contingencies, and does not, as a rule, go at his greatest pace, unless actually required to do so. He hangs back, as it were—maybe to avoid a stroke from the stag, or to look out for the proper place to seize. One hound will seize one part, one another. " Bran's point of attack was always at the shoulder or fore leg, whilst Oscar had a habit of biting at the hind leg, above the hock, frequently cutting through the flesh and tendons in an extraordinary manner, and tumbling over the deer very quickly," says St. John in his "Highland Sports."

His endurance is great, his scent keen, and Ronaldson Macdonnel, of Glengarry, instances one hound which, held in a leash, followed the track of a wounded stag, in unfavourable rainy weather, for three successive days; then the quarry was killed. The story goes, that this stag was wounded within three miles of Invergarry House, and was traced that night to the Glenmoriston. At dusk, in the evening, the stalkers placed a stone on each side of the last fresh print of his hoof, and another over it ; and this they did each night following. On the succeeding morning they removed the upper stone, when the dog recovered the scent, and the deer was that day hunted over a great part of the Glenmoriston ground. On the third day it was retraced on to Glengarry, where a shot at close quarters brought the unprecedented drag to a conclusion.

When hunting, the deerhound runs mute, as he does when coursing, but when the stag is brought to bay, the hound opens, and by his "baying" or barking, attracts his master to the spot, where, maybe, in some pool, with a steep rock at his back, the noble monarch of the glen bids defiance to his foes.

In puppyhood, the deerhound is delicate, and difficult to rear, that scourge known as distemper carrying him off in large numbers. This is, no doubt, owing to continued inbreeding, but with our increasing knowledge of canine ailments, and some slight introduction of fresh blood, which may perhaps come through the Irish wolfhound and his Great Dane cross, the mortality is decreasing.

During 1892 a club to look after the welfare of

the deerhound was established, and issued the following description of him :

Head.—The head should be broadest at the ears, tapering slightly to the eyes, with the muzzle tapering more decidedly to the nose. The muzzle should be pointed, but the teeth and lips level. The head should be long, the skull flat, rather than round, with a very slight rise over the eyes, but with nothing approaching a stop. The skull should be coated with moderately long hair, which is softer than the rest of the coat. The nose should be black (though in some blue-fawns the colour is blue), and slightly aquiline. In the lighter-coloured dogs a black muzzle is preferred. There should be a good moustache of rather silky hair, and a fair beard.

Ears.—The ears should be set on high, and, in repose, folded back like the greyhound's, though raised above the head in excitement without losing the fold, and even in some cases, semi-erect. A prick ear is bad. A big thick ear hanging flat to the head, or heavily coated with long hair, is the worst of faults. The ear should be soft, glossy, and like a mouse's coat to the touch, and the smaller it is the better. It should have no long coat or long fringe, but there is often a silky, silvery coat on the body of the ear and the tip. Whatever the general colour, the ears should be black or dark-coloured.

46

Neck and *shoulders.*—The neck should be long—
that is, of the length that befits the greyhound
character of the dog. An over-long neck is not
necessary nor desirable, for the dog is not required
to stoop to his work like a greyhound, and it must
be remembered that the mane, which every good
specimen should have, detracts from the apparent
length of neck. Moreover, a deerhound requires a
very strong neck to hold a stag. The nape of the
neck should be very prominent where the head is set
on, and the throat should be clean-cut at the angle
and prominent. The shoulders should be well
sloped, the blades well back, and not too much width
between them. Loaded and straight shoulders very
bad faults.

Stern.—Stern should be tolerably long, tapering,
and reaching to within 1½in. off the ground, and
about 1½in. below the hocks. When the dog is still,
dropped perfectly straight down, or curved. When
in motion it should be curved, when excited in no
case to be lifted out of the line of the back. It
should be well covered with hair, on the inside, thick
and wiry, underside longer, and towards the end a
slight fringe not objectionable. A curl or ring tail
very undesirable.

Eyes.—The eyes should be dark ; generally they
are dark brown or hazel. A very light eye is not

liked. The eye is moderately full, with a soft look in repose, but a keen, far-away look when the dog is roused. The rims of the eyelids should be black.

Body.—The body and general formation is that of a greyhound of larger size and bone. Chest deep rather than broad, but not too narrow and flat-sided. The loin well arched and drooping to the tail. A straight back is not desirable, this formation being unsuitable for going up-hill, and very unsightly.

Legs and *feet.*—The legs should be broad and flat, a good broad forearm and elbow being desirable. Forelegs, of course, as straight as possible. Feet close and compact, with well-arched toes. The hind quarters drooping, and as broad and powerful as possible, the hips being set wide apart. The hind legs should be well bent at the stifle, with great length from the hip to the hock, which should be broad and flat. Cow hocks, weak pasterns, straight stifles, and splay feet very bad faults.

Coat.—The hair on the body, neck, and quarters should be harsh and wiry, and about three or four inches long; that on the head, breast, and belly is much softer. There should be a slight hairy fringe on the inside of the fore and hind legs, but nothing approaching "the feather" of a colley. The deer-hound should be a shaggy dog, but not over-coated. A woolly coat is bad. Some good strains have a slight mixture of silky coat with the hard, which is preferable to a woolly coat, but the proper coat is a thick, close-lying, ragged coat, harsh or crisp to the touch.

Colour.—Colour is much a matter of fancy, but there is no manner of doubt that the dark blue-grey is the most preferred. Next comes the darker and lighter greys or brindles, the darkest being generally preferred. Yellow and sandy, red or red fawn, especially with black points, *i.e.*, ears and muzzles, are also in equal estimation, this being the colour of the oldest known strains, the M'Neil and the Chest-hill Menzies. White is condemned by all the old authorities, but a white chest and white toes, occurring as they do in a great many of the darkest coloured dogs, are not so greatly objected to, but the less the better, as the deerhound is a self-coloured dog. A white blaze on the head, or a white collar, should entirely disqualify. In other cases, though passable, yet an attempt should be made to get rid of white markings. The less white the better, but a slight white tip to the stern occurs in the best strains.

Height of dogs.—From 28in. to 30in., or even more if there be symmetry without coarseness, but which is rare.

Height of bitches.—From 26in. upwards. There

can be no objection to a bitch being large, unless too coarse, as even at her greatest height she does not approach that of a dog, and, therefore, could not have been too big for work, as over-big dogs are. Besides, a big bitch is good for breeding and keeping up the size.

Weight.—From 85lb. to 105lb. in dogs ; from 65lb. to 80lb. in bitches.

The club did not issue the numerical value of the various points, but I should place them as follows :

	Value.		Value.
Head and skull	15	Legs and feet.............	10
Eyes and ears................	10	Coat	8
Neck and chest	10	Stern	5
Body, including loins ...	10	Colour	5
Thighs and hocks :.........	12	General symmetry.......	15
	57		43

Grand Total 100.

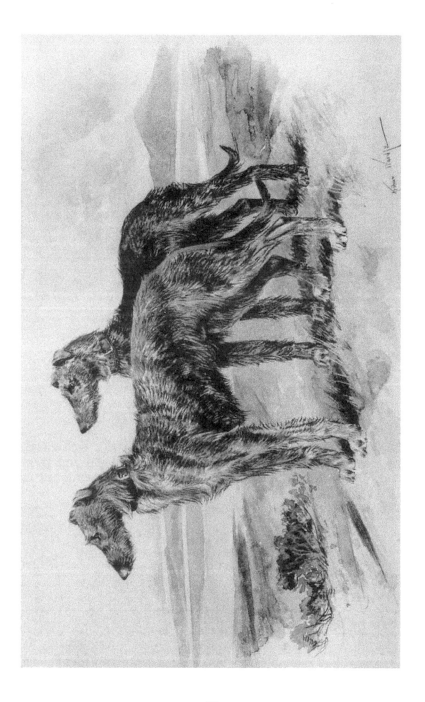

Albion L. Page's, 69 Wall Street, New York.
LOCHIEL.

THE HOUND (DEERHOUND).

ORIGIN.—Undoubtedly descended from the Irish wolfhound, though some claim it to be either a cross of foxhound and greyhound, or greyhound and bloodhound. It is first mentioned in 1528 as a distinct breed.

USES.—Hunting deer.

SCALE OF POINTS, ETC.

	Value.			Value.
Head and skull	15	Coat		8
Eyes and ears	10	Stern		5
Neck and chest	10	Color		5
Body	10	Symmetry		15
Thighs and hocks	12			
Legs and feet	10	Total		100

HEAD.—Skull resembles that of a coarse, large greyhound, long and wide between ears; stop very slight. Jaws long; teeth level and strong; nostrils open, but not very wide; cheeks muscular; bone under eye neither prominent nor hollow. Ears small, thin, carried a trifle higher than those of the greyhound, but should turn over at tips; pricked ears very objectionable; they should be thinly fringed with hair at edges only. Eyes full, and dark hazel, sometimes blue.

NECK.—Long enough to allow the dog to stoop to the scent at a fast pace.

CHEST AND SHOULDERS.—Chest deep rather than wide, resembling that of greyhound; girth of a full-size dog deerhound should be at least 2 inches greater than its height; shoulders long, oblique, and muscular.

BACK AND BACK RIBS.—Back should be powerful; a good loin should measure 25 or 26 inches; back ribs are often rather shallow, but they should be well sprung; loins arched, drooping to root of tail.

ELBOWS AND STIFLES.—Elbows well let down to give length to true arm, and quite straight; stifles wide apart, well bent.

SYMMETRY is essential to its position as a companionable dog.

QUALITY is also to be regarded as of great importance.

LEGS AND QUARTERS.—Great bone and muscle are essential; the bones must be well put together at knees and hocks, which should be long and well developed; quarters deep, but seldom wide, with considerable slope to tail.

FEET.—Well arched and cat-like.

COLOR AND COAT.—The colors are dark blue, fawn, grizzle, and brindle, the latter with more or less tint of blue; the fawn should have tips of ears dark; the grizzle generally has a decided tint of blue; white on breast or toes should not disqualify a dog. Coat is coarser on back than elsewhere, and many claim it should be intermediate between silk and wool, and not the coarse hair often met with. The whole body is clothed with a rough coat, sometimes amounting to shagginess; that of muzzle is longer in proportion than elsewhere, but the mustache should not be wiry, and should stand out in irregular tufts; there should be no approach to feather on legs, but their inside should be hairy.

TAIL.—Long and gently curved, without any twist, thinly clothed with hair only.

Mr. John E. Thayer's (Hillside Kennels, Lancaster, Mass.)
CHAMPION "CHIEFTAIN"

THE DEERHOUND

Origin.—On account of the great similarity existing between this dog and the Irish Wolfhound, there is very little doubt but that it descended from it, as claimed by so many, though there are some who contend that it is a cross either of the foxhound and greyhound, or greyhound and bloodhound. It is first mentioned as a distinct breed in 1528, while one authority asserts that the Irish Wolfhound was imported into Ireland in the VI century, B. C., and so claims it to be the parent of the deerhound.

Uses.—Hunting deer.

*STANDARD.

Head.—Broadest at the ears, tapering slightly to the eyes, with the muzzle tapering more decidedly to the nose. The muzzle should be pointed, but the teeth and lips level. The head should be long, the skull flat rather than round, with a very slight rise over the eyes, but with nothing approaching a stop. The skull should be coated with moderately long hair, which is softer than the rest of the coat. The nose should be black (though in some blue-fawns the color is blue), and slightly aquiline. In the light colored dogs, a black muzzle is preferred. There should be a good mustache of rather silky hair, and a fair beard.

Ears.—Set on high, and in repose, folded like the greyhound's, though raised above the head in excitement without losing the fold, and even in some cases semi-erect. A prick ear is bad. A big thick ear hanging flat to

54

the head, or heavily coated with long hair, is the worst of faults. The ear should be soft, glossy, and like a mouse's coat to the touch, and the smaller it is the better. It should have no long coat or long fringe, but there is often a silky silvery coat on the body of the ear and the tip. Whatever the general color, the ears should be black or dark colored.

Neck and Shoulders.—Neck long—that is, of the length that befits the greyhound character of the dog. An over-long neck is not necessary nor desirable, for the dog is not required to stoop to his work like a greyhound, and it must be remembered that the mane, which every good specimen should have, detracts from the apparent length of the neck. Moreover, a deerhound requires a very strong neck to hold a stag. The nape of the neck should be very prominent where the head is set on, and the throat should be clean-cut at the angle and prominent. The shoulders should be well sloped, the blades well back, and not too much width between them. Loaded and straight shoulders are very bad faults.

Eyes.—Dark; generally they are dark brown or hazel. A very light eye is not liked. The eye is moderately full with a soft look in repose, but a keen far-away look when the dog is roused. The rims of the eyelids should be black.

Body.—Body and general formation is that of a greyhound of larger size and bone. Chest deep rather than broad, but not too narrow and flat-sided. Loin well arched and drooping to the tail. A straight back is not desirable, this formation being unsuitable for going up hill, and very unsightly.

Mr. E. W. Murphy's (6 Rumford Place, Liverpool, Eng.)
" WINIFRED "

55

Legs and Feet.—Legs broad and flat, a good broad fore-arm and elbow being desirable. Fore-legs as straight as possible, feet close and compact, with well arched toes, the hind-quarters drooping, and as broad and powerful as possible, the hips being set well apart. Hind-legs should be well bent at the stifle, with great length from the hip to the hock, which should be broad and flat. Cow hocks, weak pasterns, straight stifles and splay feet are very bad faults.

Coat.—Hair on the body, neck, and quarters should be harsh and wiry, and about three or four inches long; that on the head, breast and belly is much softer. There should be a slight hairy fringe on the inside of the fore and hind-legs, but nothing approaching the feather of a Collie. The Deerhound should be a shaggy dog, but not over-coated. A wooly coat is bad. Some good strains have a slight mixture of silky coat with the hard, which is preferable to a wooly coat, but the proper coat is a thick, close-lying, ragged coat, harsh or crisp to the touch.

Color.—This is much a matter of fancy, but there is no manner of doubt that the dark blue grey is the most preferable. Next comes the darker and lighter greys or brindles, the darkest being generally preferred. Yellow and sandy, red or red-fawn, especially with black points, *i. e.*, ears and muzzles, are also in equal estimation. White is condemned, but a white chest and white toes, occurring as they do in many of the darkest colored dogs, are not so greatly objected to, but the less the better, as the Deerhound is a self-colored dog. A white blaze on the head, or a white collar, should entirely *disqualify*. A slight white tip to the stern occurs in the best strains.

Stern.—Tolerably long, tapering, and reaching to within one and one-half inches of the ground, and about one and one-half inches below the hocks. When the dog is still, it is dropped perfectly straight down or curved. When in motion, it should be curved; when excited, in no case to be lifted out of the line of the back. It should be well covered with hair, on the inside thick and wiry, underside longer, and towards the end a slight fringe is not objectionable. A curl or ring tail is very undesirable.

Height.—Dogs, from 28 in. to 30 in. or even more. Bitches, from 26 in. upwards.

Weight.—Dogs, from 85 lb. to 105 lb. Bitches, from 65 lb. to 80 lb.

SCALE OF POINTS.

Head and skull	15	Legs and feet	10
Eyes and ears	10	Coat	8
Neck and chest	10	Stern	5
Body, including loins	10	Color	15
Thighs and hocks	12	General symmetry	15
Total			100

COMMENTS.

Though there is a great similarity existing between the Deerhound, Greyhound and Irish Wolfhound, each is possessed of a certain individuality that distinguishes one from the other, and which should be apparent in each. The Deerhound is much heavier built than the Greyhound, is stronger in head, and not built on lines that indicate as great speed. The chest is not so deep, nor is the neck so long, as the Deerhound does not have to stoop to attack its quarry as the Greyhound does. A narrow or weak head are decided blemishes in this breed, and light eyes do not add to the beauty of the face. The nose should never be light-colored, and one so colored is decidedly "out of joint." A prick-ear is an abomination, as is a thick heavy one. Good sloping shoulders and straight legs are essentials, as no faults seem to be more objected to than crooked legs and shoulders that are heavy and out at the elbow.

As called for in the standard, the Deerhound should weigh from 85 to 105 lbs. It will be readily seen that he is a large dog, and where the limit of weight can be obtained without coarseness and lumber it is greatly to be desired. One of the greatest faults that breeders have to contend against in all the large breeds is lightness of bone, and this fault seems to be only too prevalent in the Deerhound. There are today in this country many dogs that, were they possessed of good and substantial bone, would make for themselves a record similar to that made by Mr. Thayer's great dog Chieftain, but they are sadly lacking in this respect, so much so that the deficiency is painfully apparent. Again we have a great difficulty in breeding the proper type of head, and until we can succeed in eradicating these defects we will be fighting against great odds. Another great fault that is most noticeable in the larger breeds of dogs is their not standing well on their front legs. This must be closely watched and the fault remedied if possible.

MR. ROBERT HOOD-WRIGHT'S DEER-HOUND CHAMPION SELWOOD D'HOURAN

MR. ROBERT HOOD-WRIGHT'S DEER-HOUND CHAMPION SELWOOD CALLACK

The Deerhound

Regarding the origin of the Scottish Deerhound

there is very little reliable information, though there can be no questioning the fact that it is a variety of dog indigenous to the Highlands, and bred specially for the purpose of hunting the deer.

About forty-five years since there were not many of these Hounds in England, and even in their native land at, or about, this period, they were by no means common.

Although powerful and swift dogs, they are only used to a very limited extent, and breeders of these Hounds keep them more for companionship, and exhibition purposes.

They make excellent watch-dogs, and are exceedingly hardy.

The following description is that issued by the Deerhound Club :—

Head.—The head should be broadest at the ears, tapering slightly to the eyes, with the muzzle tapering more decidedly to the nose.

The muzzle to be pointed, but the teeth and lips level.

The head ought to be long, the skull flat, rather than round, with a very slight rise over the eyes, but with nothing approaching a "stop."

The skull should be coated with moderately long hair, which is softer than the rest of the coat.

The nose to be black (although in some blue fawns the colour is blue) and slightly aquiline.

In the lighter coloured dogs a black muzzle is preferred. There should be a good moustache of rather silky hair and a fair beard.

Ears.—These to be set on "high," and in repose folded back like those of the Greyhound, though raised above the head during excitement without losing the fold, and, in some cases, semi-erect.

A "prick" ear is bad.

A big, thick ear hanging flat to the head, or

heavily coated with long hair, is one of the worst faults. The ear should be soft, glossy and like a mouse's coat to the touch, and the smaller it is, the better. It should have no long coat or long fringe, but there is often a silky, silvery coat on the body of the ear and the tip.

Whatever the general colour, the ears ought to be black, or dark coloured.

Neck and Shoulders.—The neck should be long —that is, of the length that befits the Greyhound character of the dog.

An overlong neck is neither necessary nor desirable, for the dog is not required to stoop to his work like a Greyhound, and it must be remembered that the mane, which every good specimen should have, detracts from the apparent length of the neck.

Moreover, a Deerhound requires a very strong neck to hold a stag.

The nape of the neck must be very prominent where the head is set on, and the throat clean cut at the angle, and prominent.

Shoulders to be of good slope and blades well back. Loaded and straight shoulders are faulty ones.

Stern.—To be tolerably long, tapering and reaching to within 1½ inches of the ground, and about the same distance below hocks.

When the Hound is at rest, tail ought to be quite straight down, or curved.

DEERHOUND CHAMPION ST RONAN'S RHYME (Property of
Mr HARRY RAWSON).

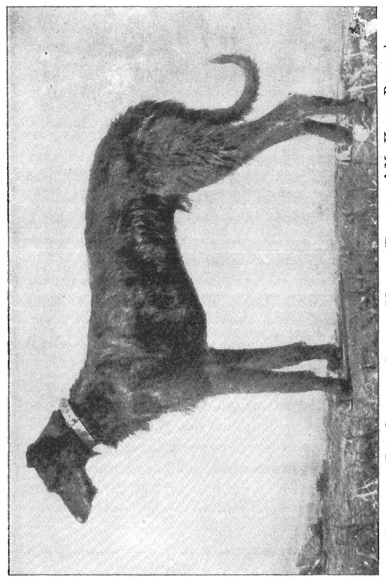

Deerhound Dog Champion Selwood Morven (Property of Mr Harry Rawson).

During excitement, curved, and in no case lifted out of the line of the back.

It should be well covered with hair on the inside, thick and woolly, underside longer, and a slight fringe near tip not objectionable. A curl or ring tail very faulty.

Eyes.—These should be dark ; generally they are dark brown or hazel. A very light eye is not liked. The eye is moderately full, with a soft look during repose, but a keen, far-away expression when the Hound is roused. Rims of eyelids ought to be black.

Body.—The body and general formation is that of a Greyhound, of larger size and bone.

Chest deep, rather than broad, but not too narrow, and flat-sided. The loin well arched, and drooping to the tail. A straight back is not desirable, this formation being unsuitable for uphill work, and very unsightly.

Legs and Feet.—The legs to be broad and flat, with good broad forearms and elbows.

Straight fore-limbs, and close compact feet.

The hind-quarters to be drooping, and as broad and powerful as possible, the hips being set wide apart.

The hind-legs to be well bent at the stifle, with great length from hips to hocks, and the latter broad and flat.

Cow-hocks, weak pasterns, straight stifles, and splay feet are the worst of faults.

Coat.—The hair on the body, neck, and quarters should be hard and wiry, and about 3 or 4 inches in length, and that on the head, breast, and belly much softer. There ought to be a slight hairy fringe on the inside of the fore and hind legs, but nothing approaching the feather of a Collie.

The Deerhound ought to be a shaggy dog, but not overcoated. A woolly coat is a bad one.

Some good strains have a mixture of silky coat with the hard, and this is preferable to a woolly coat. The proper Deerhound coat is thick, close-lying, ragged, and harsh or crisp to the feel.

Colour.—More a matter for individual fancy.

A dark blue-grey most preferred, and after this, darker and lighter grey, or brindles, the darkest being preferred.

Yellow, sandy-red, or red-fawn, with black points (*i.e.*, ears and muzzle), are equally esteemed, more so because two of the oldest strains—the M'Neil and Chesthill Menzies—are of these colours.

White is condemned by all the old authorities, but a white chest and white toes, occurring as they do in a great many of the darkest coloured dogs, are not so much objected to, though less the better, as the Deerhound is a self-coloured dog.

A white blaze on the head, or a white collar, should entirely *disqualify.*

A white tip on tail occurs in most strains.

Height of Dogs.—From 28 to 30 inches.

Height of Bitches.—From 26 inches upwards.

A big bitch is better for breeding and keeping up size. Ought not to exceed the height of the dog under any circumstances.

Weight.—Dogs, 85 to 105 lbs. Bitches, 65 to 80 lbs.

Mr Rawson, of Joppa, kindly supplied me with photographs.

THE TOTAL POINTS REQUIRED FOR A DEERHOUND

Character—

Length and shape of head . .	10
Ears	6
Beard and eyebrows . . .	3
Eyes	5
Coat	7
Neck	5
Tail	4
Nails	2
Teeth	5
	—47

Body—

Height at shoulder . . .	10
Substance and girth . . .	9
Length and symmetry of body .	9
	—28

Limbs—

Loins and hocks . . .	10
Fore-limbs	8
Feet	7
	—25
Total . . .	100

THE DEERHOUND.

BY ROBERT LEIGHTON.

"A chieftain's, in good truth, this dog was once.
And if in form and action he remained
What he then was when first Odysseus left,
His swiftness and his strength would well have roused
Thy wonder at his hunting : never game
Escaped him in the thickest woodland glade :
Whatever he might follow, by their trail
He knew them all most thoroughly."

—CORDREY'S "ODYSSEY."

THE Deerhound is one of the most decorative of dogs, impressively stately and picturesque wherever he is seen, whether it be amid the surroundings of the baronial hall, reclining at luxurious length before the open hearth in the fitful light of the log fire that flickers on polished armour and tarnished tapestry ; out in the open, straining at the leash as he scents the dewy air, or gracefully bounding over the purple of his native hills. Grace and majesty are in his every movement and attitude, and even to the most prosaic mind there is about him the inseparable glamour of feudal romance and poetry. He is at his best alert in the excitement of the chase ; but all too rare now is the inspiring sight that once was common among the mountains of Morven and the glens of Argyll of the deep-voiced hound speeding in pursuit of his antlered prey, racing him at full stretch along the mountain's ridge, or baying him at last in the fastness of darksome corrie or deep ravine. Gone are the good romantic days of stalking, beloved by Scrope. The Highlands have lost their loneliness, and the inventions of the modern gunsmith have robbed one of the grandest of hunting dogs of his glory, relegating him to the life of a pedestrian pet, whose highest dignity is the winning of a pecuniary prize under Kennel Club rules.

Historians of the Deerhound associate him with the original Irish Wolfdog, of whom he is obviously a close relative, and it is sure that when the wolf still lingered in the land it was the frequent quarry of the Highland as of the Hibernian hound. Legend has it that Prince Ossian, son of Fingal, King of Morven, hunted the wolf with the grey, long-bounding dogs. "Swift-footed Luath " and "White-breasted Bran " are among the names of Ossian's hounds. I am disposed to affirm that the old Irish Wolfhound and the Highland Deerhound are not only intimately allied in form and nature, but that they are two strains of an identical breed, altered only in size by circumstance and environment. There are reasons for the supposition that they were originally of one family. During the period of the Danish dominion over the Hebrides, the sport-loving Scandinavians held such constant communication between Scotland and Ireland that it is to be presumed they commonly interbred the hounds of both countries.

Nor was the process confined to one channel of intercourse. In the southern parts of the main island, and particularly in Wessex, there existed in ancient times a rough-coated Gazehound of analogous type, which possibly drifted over the border to become more rugged and sturdy under the influence of a rigorous climate. The dogs of Great Britain have never for long remained strictly local in type and character. Civil wars, the courtesies of friendly kings, and

68

extensive hunting expeditions have all had their effect in the work of distribution. King Arthur and his noble knights of the Round Table—all of them imbued with enthusiasm for the chase—were experts in the knowledge of hunting dogs, and they took their hounds with them wherever they went.

distinct from its now larger Irish relative, it was recognised as a native dog in Scotland in very early times, and it was distinguished as being superior in strength and beauty to the hounds of the Picts. Stewart in his "Buik of the Cronicles of Scotland" * quaintly records that

SCENE AT ABBOTSFORD.
SIR WALTER SCOTT'S MAIDA AND TORRUM.
FROM THE PAINTING BY SIR EDWIN LANDSEER, R.A.

It is difficult, even with the help of illuminated manuscripts and the records of contemporary scribes, to determine the particular breeds most in vogue; but King Arthur's Cavall and the yet more famous Hodain were almost certainly of a rough Greyhound type. Hodain himself—the hound who shared the love potion with Sir Tristram and Iseult—was brought by the knight of Lyonesse over from Ireland, a gift from King Anguish of that land, and was presumably of the breed we are now considering. There is nothing more probable than that in the days of chivalry hounds were numbered among the presents given by king to king.

Whatever the source of the Highland Deerhound, and at whatever period it became

"The Pictis houndis were nocht of sic speed
As Scottis houndis, nor yet sae gude at need,
Nor in sic game they were nocht half sae gude,
Nor of sic pleasure, nor sic pulchritude."

The reference is included in the description of a battle fought on account of a Deerhound. The hound's name is not given, but he is said to have excelled all others "sae far as into licht the moon does near a star." He was the property of a Scots king who had been enjoying a great hunting

* This was a metrical version of Hector Boece's History, which was written in Latin and published in Paris in 1526-7. The translation was made in 1531 by command of Margaret, Queen of James the Fourth.

CH. TALISMAN BY CH. ST. RONAN'S RANGER—CH. CRAIGIE.
BRED AND OWNED BY MRS. H. ARMSTRONG.
Photograph by Russell.

in the Grampians among the Picts, who coveted the dog. To console them the king made them a gift of a pair of his hounds, but, not wholly content, they stole his favourite. The thieves were pursued, and a bloody battle followed, in which sixty good Scots and a hundred Picts were slain, before the dog was restored to his rightful owner.

From that time onward, Scottish nobles cherished their strains of Deerhound, seeking glorious sport in the Highland forests. In Pitscottie's " History of Scotland " (1528) it is said that " the King desired all gentlemen that had dogges that war guid to bring theme to hunt in the saides boundis quhilk the most pairt of the noblemen of the Highlands did, such as the Earles of Huntlie, Argyle, and Athole, who brought their Deerhoundes with theme and hunted with his majestie." The red deer belonged by inexorable law to the kings of Scotland, and great drives, which often lasted for several days, were made to round up the herds into given neighbourhoods for the pleasure of the court, as in the reign of

Queen Mary. But the organised coursing of deer by courtiers ceased during the Stuart troubles, and was left to servants, the pursuit of men being regarded as more suitable for the occupation of a gentleman.

At the time when Dr. Johnson made his tour in the Hebrides, deer hunting was still mainly in the hands of retainers, who thus replenished their chief's larder. " The stags of the mountains are less than those of our parks and forests," wrote Johnson, with reference to sport in the Isle of Skye. " The deer are not driven with horns and hounds. A sportsman, with his gun in his hand, watches the animal, and when he has wounded him, traces him by the blood. They have a race of brindled Greyhounds, larger and stronger than those with which we course hares, and these are the only dogs used by them for the chase." Boswell mentions that Mr. Grant, of Glenmoriston, permitted any stranger to range his forest after deer, in the belief that nobody could do them any injury. The stag was valued only for the amount of venison it might yield. The abandonment of the sport and the gradual disappearance of the boar and the wolf naturally caused the Deerhound to decline both in number and in size and strength, and by the end of the eighteenth century the breed had become scarce.

The revival of deerstalking dates back hardly further than a hundred years. It reached its greatest popularity in the Highlands at the time when the late Queen and Prince Albert were in residence at Balmoral. Solomon, Hector, and Bran were among the Balmoral hounds. Bran was an especially fine animal—one of the best of his time, standing over thirty inches in height. It was at this period that Sir Edwin Landseer was industriously transferring to canvas his admiration of the typical Deerhound. Sir Walter Scott had already done much to preserve public interest in the breed, both by his writings and by the fact that he kept many of these dogs at Abbotsford ; but it is saddening to note that although his Torrum was the son of a true Glengarry sire, yet his famous Maida was a mongrel by a Pyrenean Wolfdog. Notwithstanding the sinister bend, however, Maida was a magnificent animal, partaking of the appearance of his Deerhound dam, but having height and power from his sire. The cross was of benefit to the breed, and from Maida many of our best modern Deerhounds are descended. Washington Irving described him as a giant in iron grey. Landseer's portrait of him (p. 169) shows him to have been a white dog with a grey saddle mingled with black, extending into patches on the thighs. He had a white blaze up the face, and a white muzzle and collar, and his dark ears seem to have been cropped. The companion hound sitting behind him in the picture is of better type.

Scrope's neglected but delightful book on deerstalking was written when the sport was at its zenith, and it contains fascinating descriptions of the glories of pursuing the red deer in the wilds of the forest of Atholl, and of the performances of such hounds as Tarff and Derig and Schuloch.

The Deerhounds were used in two ways. In the one case they coursed the deer from first to last without the aid of man. In the other, they held the wounded stag at bay. In the former case a hound of superior strength, speed, and courage was required. So soon as the herd were in sight, the hunters, getting as near as they could, slipped the hounds and the race began. On the roughest ground the strong-legged, hard-footed dogs could hold their own, while on the flat they overhauled their quarry. They stuck staunchly to the chase, and when within seizing distance would sometimes spring at the leg in order to confuse and encumber the stag until there came a better opportunity of springing at the neck. If the stag stood at bay, woe betide the hound whose courage led him to make a frontal attack ; for he would surely pay for his valour with his life or sustain terrible injuries. If, however, the attack was made from behind, the hunter would generally come up to find the deer dead, while the hounds were unharmed. Their duty was not to kill their victim but to keep him at bay until the hunters arrived.

Two historic feats of strength and endurance illustrate the tenacity of the Deerhound at work. A brace of half-bred dogs, named Percy and Douglas, the property of Mr. Scrope, kept a stag at bay from Saturday

CH. BLAIR ATHOL BY CH. SELWOOD DHOURAN——KATRINE.
BRED AND OWNED BY MRS. W. C. GREW.

71

night to Monday morning; and the pure bred Bran by himself pulled down two unwounded stags, one carrying ten and the other eleven tines. These, of course, are record performances, but they demonstrate the possibilities of the Deerhound when trained to his natural sport.

In Scrope's time driving was commonly resorted to in the extensive forests, but nowadays when forests are sub-divided into limited shootings the deer are seldom moved from their home preserves, whilst with the use of improved telescopes and the small-bore rifle, stalking has gone out of fashion. With guns having a muzzle velocity of 2,500 feet per second, it is no longer necessary for sportsmen stealthily to stalk their game to come within easy range, and as for dogs, they have become so doubtful an appendage to the chase that we have an experienced deerstalker like Cameron of Lochiel soberly putting the question : " Ought dogs to be used in a forest at all ? " *

Obviously they ought still to be of use in enabling the sportsman to secure his wounded deer, which may not be crippled beyond the possibility of successful flight. Admitting that dogs are thus helpful in tracking, Cameron of Lochiel discusses the question as to the breed best adapted for this sport, and, with all a Highlander's love for the Deerhound, he yet reluctantly decides that these magnificent dogs are not by any means the most suitable. " For use on the hill," he adds, " nothing beats the Collie. He is possessed of instinct—one may almost call it sense—in a higher degree than any other breed, and he is more tractable—he will run by sight or by scent, loose or on a cord ; he will keep close to his master, requiring no gillie to lead him ; he can be taught to lie down, and will even learn to crawl when necessary ; and at any rate his motions are those of an animal who knows that he is trying to approach a prey unobserved. But the chief merit in a Collie over all other dogs for following a

* " The Red Deer." Fur and Feather Series (Longman and Co., 1896).

wounded deer consists in his wonderful faculty for distinguishing between the track of a wounded and that of a cold stag."

Primarily and essentially the Deerhound belongs to the order *Agaseus*, hunting by sight and not by scent, and although he may indeed occasionally put his nose to the ground, yet his powers of scent are not remarkable. His vocation, therefore, has undergone a change, and it was recently ascertained that of sixty deer forests there were only six upon which Deerhounds were kept for sporting purposes.

Happily the Deerhound has suffered no decline in the favour bestowed upon him for his own sake. The contrary is rather the case, and he is still an aristocrat among dogs, valued for his good looks, the symmetry of his form, his grace and elegance, and even more so for his faithful and affectionate nature. Sir Walter Scott declared that he was " a most perfect creature of heaven," and when one sees him represented in so beautiful a specimen of his noble race as St. Ronan's Rhyme, for example, or Talisman, or Ayrshire, one is tempted to echo this high praise.

In recent years the Deerhound has been fashionable at exhibitions of dogs, and although the number brought into competition is never very great, yet it is always apparent that the true type is being steadily preserved and that in many respects decided improvements are achieved. The oldest strain is probably that of Chesthill, on Loch Tay, established by the Menzies over a hundred years ago. It is no longer kept in its integrity by the Menzies family, but Mr. R. Hood Wright, whose name must always be intimately associated with this breed, came into possession of some of the strain, and bred from them to a considerable extent. Mr. G. W. Hickman, of Selly Hill, made similar efforts, his Morni and Garry being of true Chesthill descent. Cameron of Lochiel had also a venerable strain, of which his Torrum, exhibited at Birmingham in 1869, was a notable example. Other strains which have entered largely into our present day Deerhounds are those of Morrison of Glenelg, McNeil of Colonsay,

72

THE DEER DRIVE.

FROM THE PAINTING BY SIR EDWIN LANDSEER, R.A., IN THE ROYAL COLLECTION.

73

and Bateson of Cambusmere; the last mentioned providing the originals of some of the paintings by Landseer, who considered them the finest Deerhounds he had ever seen. The Marquis of Breadalbane also owned a famous strain on the Black Mount Forest, as did Lord Campbell of Glendarule. The hounds kept at Windsor were usually of splendid type. Three of these, including the magnificent dog Keildar

grand specimen of his race, strong framed, with plenty of hair of a blue brindle colour. Captain Graham's own dog Keildar, who had been trained for deerstalking in Windsor Park, was perhaps one of the most elegant and aristocratic-looking Deerhounds ever seen. His full height was 30 inches, girth 33½ inches, and weight, 95 lbs., his colour bluish fawn, slightly brindled, the muzzle and ears being blue. His nearest competitor

HEAD OF CH. BLAIR ATHOL.

and his sister Hag, came nto the hands of Captain G. A. Graham, of Dursley, who is still one of our greatest authorities on the Deerhound.

Five-and-twenty years ago Captain Graham drew up a list of the most notable dogs of the last century. Among these were Sir St. George Gore's Gruim (1843-44), Black Bran (1850-51); the Marquis of Breadalbane's King of the Forest, said to stand 33 inches high; Mr. Beasley's Alder (1863-67), bred by Sir John McNeil of Colonsay; Mr. Donald Cameron's Torrum (1869), and his two sons Monzie and Young Torrum; and Mr. Dadley's Hector, who was probably the best-bred dog living in the early 'eighties. Torrum, however, appears to have been the most successful of these dogs at stud. He was an exceedingly

for perfection was, after Hector, probably Mr. Hood Wright's Bevis, a darkish red brown brindle of about 29 inches. Mr. Wright was the breeder of Champion Selwood Morven, who was the celebrity of his race about 1897, and who became the property of Mr. Harry Rawson, of Joppa House, Midlothian. This stately dog was a dark heather brindle, standing 32⅜ inches at the shoulder, with a chest girth of 34½ inches.

A few years ago breeders were inclined to mar the beauty of the Deerhound by a too anxious endeavour to obtain great size rather than to preserve the genuine type; but this error has been sufficiently corrected, with the result that symmetry and elegance conjoined with the desired attributes of speed are not sacrificed. The qualities

74

aimed at now are a height of something less than 30 inches, and a weight not greater than 105 lbs., with straight fore-legs and short, cat-like feet, a deep chest, with broad, powerful loins, slightly arched, and strength of hind-quarters, with well-bent stifles, and the hocks well let down. Straight stifles are objectionable, giving a stilty appearance. Thick shoulders are equally a blemish to be avoided, as also a too great heaviness of bone. The following is the accepted standard of merit.

THE PERFECT DEERHOUND.

1. Head.—The head should be broadest at the ears, tapering slightly to the eyes, with the muzzle tapering more decidedly to the nose. The muzzle should be pointed, but the teeth and lips level. The head should be long, the skull flat rather than round, with a very slight rise over the eyes, but with nothing approaching a stop. The skull should be coated with moderately long hair, which is softer than the rest of the coat. The nose should be black (though in some blue-fawns the colour is blue), and slightly aquiline. In the lighter-coloured dogs a black muzzle is preferred. There should be a good moustache of rather silky hair, and a fair beard.

2. Ears.—The ears should be set on high, and, in repose, folded back like the Greyhound's, though raised above the head in excitement without losing the fold, and even, in some cases, semi-erect. A prick ear is bad. A big, thick ear, hanging flat to the head, or heavily coated with long hair, is the worst of faults. The ear should be soft, glossy, and like a mouse's coat to the touch, and the smaller it is the better. It should have no long coat or long fringe, but there is often a silky, silvery coat on the body of the ear and the tip. Whatever the general colour, the ears should be black or dark-coloured.

3. Neck and Shoulders.—The neck should be long—that is, of the length that befits the Greyhound character of the dog. An over-long neck is not necessary, nor desirable, for the dog is not required to stoop to his work like a Greyhound, and it must be remembered that the mane, which every good specimen should have, detracts from the apparent length of neck. Moreover, a Deerhound requires a very strong neck to hold a stag. The nape of the neck should be very prominent where the head is set on, and the throat should be clean-cut at the angle and prominent. The shoulders should be well sloped, the blades well back, with not too much width between them. Loaded and straight shoulders are very bad faults.

4. Stern.—Stern should be tolerably long. tapering, and reaching to within $1\frac{1}{2}$ inches of the ground, and about $1\frac{1}{2}$ inches below the hocks. When the dog is still, dropped perfectly straight down, or curved. When in motion it should be curved when excited, in no case to be lifted out of the line of the back. It should be well covered with hair, on the inside thick and wiry. underside longer, and towards the end a slight fringe is not objectionable. A curl or ring tail is very undesirable.

5. Eyes.—The eyes should be dark : generally they are dark brown or hazel. A very light eye is not liked. The eye is moderately full, with a soft look in repose, but a keen, far-away gaze when the dog is roused. The rims of the eyelids should be black.

6. Body.—The body and general formation is that of a Greyhound of larger size and bone. Chest deep rather than broad, but not too narrow and flat-sided. The loin well arched and drooping to the tail. A straight back is not desirable, this formation being unsuitable for going up-hill, and very unsightly.

7. Legs and Feet.—The legs should be broad and flat, a good broad forearm and elbow being desirable. Fore-legs, of course, as straight as possible. Feet close and compact, with well-arched toes. The hind-quarters drooping, and as broad and powerful as possible, the hips being set wide apart. The hind-legs should be well bent at the stifle, with great length from the hip to the hock, which should be broad and flat. Cow hocks, weak pasterns, straight stifles, and splay feet are very bad faults.

8. Coat.—The hair on the body, neck, and quarters should be harsh and wiry, and about 3 inches or 4 inches long ; that on the head, breast, and belly is much softer. There should be a slight hairy fringe on the inside of the fore- and hind-legs, but nothing approaching to the feathering of a Collie. The Deerhound should be a shaggy dog, but not over coated. A woolly coat is bad. Some good strains have a slight mixture of silky coat with the hard, which is preferable to a woolly coat, but the proper covering is a thick, close-lying, ragged coat, harsh or crisp to the touch.

9. Colour.—Colour is much a matter of fancy. But there is no manner of doubt that the dark blue-grey is the most preferred. Next come the darker and lighter greys or brindles, the darkest being generally preferred. Yellow and sandy-red or red-fawn, especially with black points—*i.e.*, ears and muzzle—are also in equal estimation, this being the colour of the oldest known strains, the McNeil and the Chesthill Menzies. White is condemned by all the old authorities, but a white chest and white toes, occurring as they do in a great many of the darkest-coloured dogs, are not so greatly objected to, but the less the better, as the Deerhound is a self-coloured dog. A white blaze on the head or a white collar should entirely disqualify. In other cases, though passable, yet an attempt should be made to get rid of white markings. The less white the better, but a slight white tip to the stern occurs in the best strains.

10. Height of Dogs.—From 28 inches to 30 inches, or even more if there be symmetry without coarseness, which, however, is rare.

11. Height of Bitches.—From 26 inches upwards. There can be no objection to a bitch being large, unless she is too coarse, as even at her greatest height she does not approach that of the dog, and, therefore, could not well be too big for work, as over-big dogs are. Besides, a big bitch is good for breeding and keeping up the size.

12. Weight.—From 85 pounds to 105 pounds in dogs ; from 65 pounds to 80 pounds in bitches.

Among the more prominent owners of Deerhounds at the present time are Mrs. H. Armstrong, of Jesmond, near Newcastle ; Mrs. W. C. Grew, of Knowle, Warwickshire ; Mrs. Janvrin Dickson, of Bushey Heath ; Mr. Harry Rawson, of Joppa; and Mr. H. McLauchlin, of Dublin. Mrs. Armstrong is the breeder of a beautiful dog hound in Ch. Talisman, and of two typically good bitches in Fair Maid of Perth and Bride of Lammermoor. Mrs. Grew counts as her "friends" many admirable specimens, among them being Ch. Blair Athol, Ayrshire, Kenilworth, and Ferraline. Ayrshire is considered by some judges to be the most perfect Deerhound of his sex exhibited for some time past. He is somewhat large, perhaps, but he is throughout a hound of excellent quality and character, having a most typical head, with lovely eyes and expression, perfect front feet and hindquarters. Other judges would give the palm to Mr. Harry Rawson's Ch. St. Ronan's Ranger, who is certainly difficult to excel in all the characteristics most desirable in the breed.

Mr. Harry Rawson inherits an active interest in the Deerhound. From his boyhood he has been associated with one of the most successful kennels of the breed in the kingdom ; and the St. Ronan's prefix is to be found in the pedigrees of many of the best Deerhounds in the Stud Book. To him belongs the honour of having bred what is acknowledged to be not only the least assailable of her distinguished breed now living, but possibly the most flawless Deerhound of any time in Ch. St. Ronan's Rhyme. In the attempt to accord to this remarkable bitch the position which is her due, one can only refer to her achievements. One assumes that, if anywhere, the best dogs in the kingdom are to be seen at the show held annually by the Kennel Club at the Crystal Palace, and that the chosen judges on these occasions are unbiassed and unimpeachable. A customary event at this show is that of the general competition among dogs having full championship honours in their respective breeds, and the winning dog thus becomes veritably a champion of champions. It is the severest test of merit and breeding to which a dog is ever submitted. St. Ronan's Rhyme went through the ordeal in October, 1906, and she met with conspicuous success.

This triumph of St. Ronan's Rhyme was repeated a few days afterwards at the Edinburgh show of the Scottish Kennel Club, under different judges, when again she was awarded the laurel bestowed upon the best dog in the show.

Some forty or fifty years ago the Deerhound seems to have been in danger of degeneration, and to have declined in size and stamina, and there is no doubt that the various out-crosses which were tried at that time have been of permanent profit to the breed. Sir Walter Scott's Maida was, as we have seen, the offspring of a Glengarry dam and a Pyrenean sire, who was probably responsible for the admixture of white in Maida's coat, and for the white markings which even to this day are occasionally revealed. But the sturdy dog of the Pyrenees contributed materially to the strength of the Deerhound, and all other traces of his different type and characteristics disappeared in three generations. So, too, the cross from the Russian Borzoi, which was judiciously used half a century ago, imparted to the Deerhound a degree of quality, and a certain bloodlike look, with regained symmetry of shape and grace of action, which the breed was fast losing.

For the following additional notes on the Deerhound I am indebted to Mrs. H. Armstrong.

"Though fast disappearing from the annals of hunting, the Deerhound is a great favourite to-day as a household pet and personal after the style of the Royal beast, the lion, who appears to look over the heads, or actually through the bodies, of his admiring visitors at the Zoo, into the back of beyond.

"Unfortunately, the Deerhound is to-day

THE CHAMPION OF CHAMPIONS ST. RONAN'S RHYME
(BORN FEBRUARY 23RD, 1903) BY ST RONAN'S RANGER—GINAGACH.
THIS BEAUTIFUL BITCH, THE PROPERTY OF HER BREEDER HARRY RANSON, ESQ. OF JOPPA HOUSE,
MIDLOTHIAN IS PROBABLY THE MOST PERFECT DOG OF ANY BREED AT PRESENT LIVING
Photograph by Russell.

companion, and well worthy is he of his place ; for not only is he wondrous gentle for his great size, but he is faithful, sensible, and quiet. The latter quality, indeed, may almost be described as a fault, for except for his formidable size and appearance, which strikes terror into the hearts of evildoers, he cannot be said to be a good watch, inasmuch as he will either welcome all comers as personal friends, or he will of his dignity and stateliness overlook the approach of strangers, something a most delicate and difficult dog to rear. Perhaps this is due to the extraordinary amount of inbreeding which has been so largely resorted to in this race. In order, probably, to keep the type and character, as also the pure lineage, we have the same names occurring over and over again in the same pedigree, and of those of the present day none appears more often or more surely than that of Ch. Swift—a hound bred by Mr. Singer, of Frome, Somerset, and who in turn is by Ch. Athole, the property of

77

CH. TALISMAN, BRIDE OF LAMMERMOOR AND FAIR MAID OF PERTH.
BRED AND OWNED BY MRS. H. ARMSTRONG.
Photograph by Russell.

Mr. Goulter, from a very famous bitch, Hedwig. Swift is described as a red brindle, 30½ inches at the shoulder, and possessing in a marked degree, those most desirable points, size and quality. Before him again we have Ch. Fingall II., another ancestral dignitary. He is described as being the most noted Deerhound of his day. He was not only an excellent dog at the deer, but a winner of more first prizes than any Deerhound then living. He was a very dark blue in colour.

"Another celebrated hound was Ch. Selwood Dhouran, by Ch. Swift. This was an immense dog, said by his owner, Mr. R. Hood Wright, to weigh over 100 lbs., and to stand 31 inches at the shoulder. Ch. Selwood Morven, also bred by Mr. Hood Wright, was another enormous hound, standing 32⅝ inches at the shoulder, while in girth he measured 34½ inches. Many of the old breeders assert that this is too large, and that the present day craze for size is not in accordance with what used to be considered correct in the old days of exhibiting and hunting. For instance in 1859 the representative dog chosen by " Stonehenge,"

viz. : Buscar, was 28 inches, and in 1872 the following hounds measured :—

Dogs.	Inches.	Bitches.	Inches.
Charlie	27½	Braie	27
Arran	29¾	Luffra	26
Colin	28	Hilda	26
Morna	30	Meg	26
Torrum	30	Bertha	26
Bruce	28	Juno	26
Oscar	28	Hylda	29
Young Torrum	30¼	Brenda	28
Bismarck	28		
Oscar	28		
Warrior	28		
Young Warrior	28		
Roswell	28		
Aitkin	28		

" So that four out of fourteen dogs were over 28 inches high, and three out of eight bitches over 26 inches.

"Personally, I think a dog of 30 inches a very fair size, and it is unnecessary to strive after anything taller, for about this height we generally get the better type, character and quality, while dogs taller than this have a tendency to appear coarse and heavy at

78

the shoulders, and lean too much to the Irish Wolfhound; but there is little doubt that size will always be a subject of discussion amongst Deerhound breeders, although, in the standard of points, as laid down by the Club, dogs are given as from 28 inches to 30 inches, and bitches from 26 inches upwards.

"In conclusion, let me add that I think 'once a Deerhound lover, always a Deerhound lover,' for there is something about the breed which is particularly attractive; they are no fools, if brought up sensibly, and they are obedient, while, for all they are so large, it is astonishing what little room they occupy: they have a happy knack of curling themselves up into wonderfully small compass, and lying out of the way. They do not require a very great amount of food, and are readily and easily exercised, as, if let loose in some field or other convenient place, they soon gallop themselves tired. They are as a rule excellent followers, either in town or country, keeping close to heel and walking in a dignified manner; while, on the approach of a strange dog, a slight raising of the head and tail is generally all the notice they deign to give that they have even seen the passing canine."

CHAMPION TEAM OF MR. HARRY RAWSON'S DEERHOUNDS,
REGIUS, RHYME, RODERICK, AND RANGER.

79

DEERHOUNDS.

WHILST one of the most intelligent and devoted, the Deerhound is one of the handsomest and most elegant of all breeds of dogs.

As to the antiquity of the breed there can be no question; and there is every probability that the "rough Greyhounds" used by the Anglo-Saxons to secure the Wild Boar, the Wolf, the Hart and the various kinds of "deer" were Deerhounds. Buffon says that undoubted proof remains that the race has been well known for centuries. Unfortunately, it is often difficult to trace the breed in the early literature owing to the different names which have been given to it from time to time, as for instance, "Irish Wolf Dog," "Scotch Greyhound," "Rough Greyhounds," and "Highland Deerhounds." Under the heading "Scottish Greyhound," Lieut.-Col. Charles Hamilton Smith says (in the "Naturalists' Library," edited by Sir William Jardine): "Is of the same race as the Russian, and similarly coloured ; but from greater attention, or the cross of a Stag Hound at some period, it is endowed with higher faculties of intellect, and formerly had so good a nose, that we believe this variety was mostly used as a Bloodhound." Sir Walter Scott's celebrated dog Maida was of this breed. Bewick, in his *History of Quadrupeds*, refers to the breed under the heading : "The Scottish Highland Greyhound" or "Wolf Dog." Many writers have endeavoured to show that the Deerhound is the product of the Wolf Dog of Ireland. But there would seem to be little doubt that the reverse is the case, and that the Irish Wolfhound owes a great deal

CH. ST. RONAN'S RANGER.

to the breed under discussion. The Deerhound and the Greyhound have many characteristics in common, and they probably have a common ancestor. Some writers have suggested that the present-day dog is a cross between a Greyhound and a Foxhound or a Bloodhound. Mr. Rawdon B. Lee very properly corrects this idea and adds : "If the Deerhound is to be found in greater numbers now than previously, it is only because more attention is paid to his breeding, and because the many strains that a hundred years and more ago were in the out-of-the-way places of the Highlands have, by better communication, been brought within the radius of canine admirers." The Deerhound used to be employed, not only for deer-stalking but also for coursing ; and this different use doubtless gave rise to various strains of the breed. Deer-stalking in this country is now rarely, if ever, engaged in ; and the Deerhound is kept, now-a-days, merely as a companion or for exhibition, although he is as game as ever, and is death on hares and rabbits.

The possession of a Deerhound, in days of old, was a sign of " rank." Amongst the retinues of the old Highland Chieftains this devoted animal had always a place. And so greatly was the breed valued that a " fine " of a leash of Deerhounds was the equivalent of a large sum of money, and was sometimes imposed in lieu of a long term of imprisonment. In fact, a fine of ten of these dogs has, on one occasion, gone towards expiating the crime of murder. For we learn (thanks to the researches amongst old manuscripts made by the Rev. T. W. Sneyd, a learned Staffordshire antiquary) that about the year 800 "a murder was committed in King Solomon's Hollow and the culprit on conviction was ordered to pay a fine of 200 Marks, 10 Deerhounds and 10 Hawks." Of those who have written on the Deerhound mention must always be made of the late Edwin Weston Bell, and Capt. McNeill of Colonsay ; and those interested in the breed should not fail to read the former's book on " The Scottish Deerhound " and the latter's article in William Scrope's famous work " The Days of Deer-Stalking."

The description of the breed, as adopted by the Deerhound Club, was drawn up by Mr. G. W. Hickman and that enthusiastic stalwart of the cult—Mr. R. Hood Wright. It is much to be regretted that the latter is no longer in this country. To him the present day lovers of the hound will readily accede the pride of place as the foremost breeder of the last quarter of a century ; and there are few kennels of any pretensions to-day that do not contain

some of the famous "Selwood" strain.   The description is
as follows :—

Head—The head should be broadest at the ears, tapering
slightly to the eyes, with the muzzle tapering more decidedly
to the nose.   The muzzle should be pointed, but the teeth
and lips level.   The head should be long, the skull flat
rather than round, with a very slight rise over the eyes, but
with nothing approaching a stop.   The skull should be coated
with moderately long hair, which is softer than the rest of the
coat.   The nose should be black (though in some blue-fawns
the colour is blue), and slightly aquiline.   In the lighter-
coloured dogs a black muzzle is preferred.   There should be
a good moustache of rather silky hair, and a fair beard.
Ears—The ears should be set on high, and, in repose, folded
back like the Greyhound's, though raised above the head in
excitement without losing the fold, and even in some cases
semi-erect.   A prick ear is bad.   A big thick ear hanging
flat to the head, or heavily coated with long hair, is the
worst of faults.   The ear should be soft, glossy, and like a
mouse's coat to the touch, and the smaller it is the better.
It should have no long coat or long fringe, but there is often
a silky, silvery coat on the body of the ear and the tip.
Whatever the general colour, the ears should be black or
dark-coloured.—*Neck and Shoulders*—The neck should be
long—that is of the length that befits the Greyhound
character of the dog.   An over-long neck is not necessary
nor desirable, for the dog is not required to stoop to his
work like a Greyhound, and it must be remembered that the
mane, which every good specimen should have, detracts from
the apparent length of neck.   Moreover, a Deerhound requires
a very strong neck to hold a stag.   The nape of the neck
should be very prominent where the head is set on, and the
throat should be clean cut at the angle and prominent.
The shoulders should be well sloped, the blades well back

CH. SELWOOD MORVEN.

84

and not too much width between them. Loaded and straight shoulders very bad faults.—*Stern*—Stern should be tolerably long, tapering, and reaching to within 1½ in. off the ground, and about 1½ in. below the hocks. When the dog is still, dropped perfectly straight down or curved. When in motion it should be curved when excited, in no case to be lifted out of the line of the back. It should be well covered with hair, on the inside, thick and wiry, underside longer, and towards the end a slight fringe not objectionable. A curl or ring tail very undesirable.—*Eyes*—The eyes should be dark; generally they are dark brown or hazel. A very light eye is not liked. The eye is moderately full, with a soft look in repose, but a keen, far-away look when the dog is roused. The rims of the eyelids should be black.—*Body*—The body and general formation is that of a Greyhound of larger size and bone. Chest deep rather than broad, but not too narrow and flat-sided. The loin well arched and drooping to the tail. A straight back is not desirable, this formation being unsuitable for going uphill, and very unsightly.—*Legs and Feet*—The legs should be broad and flat, and good broad forearm and elbow being desirable. Forelegs, of course, as straight as possible. Feet close and compact, with well-arranged toes. The hind quarters drooping, and as broad and powerful as possible, the hips being set wide apart. The hind legs should be well bent at the stifle, with great length from the hip to the hock, which should be broad and flat. Cow hocks, weak pasterns, straight stifles, and splay feet very bad faults.—*Coat*—The hair on the body, neck and quarters should be harsh and wiry, and about three or four inches long; that on the head, breast and belly is much softer. There should be a slight hairy fringe on the inside of the fore and hind legs, but nothing approaching the "feather" of a collie. The Deerhound should be a shaggy dog, but not overcoated. A woolly coat is bad. Some good strains have a mixture of silky coat with the hard, which is preferable to a woolly coat; but the proper coat is a thick,

close-lying, ragged coat, harsh or crisp to the touch.—
Colour—Colour is much a matter of fancy. But there is
no manner of doubt that the dark blue-grey is the most
preferred. Next comes the darker and lighter greys or
brindles, the darkest being generally preferred. Yellow and
sandy red or red fawn, especially with black points, *i.e.*,
ears and muzzles, are also in equal estimation, this being
the colour of the oldest known strains, the M'Neill and
Chesthill Menzies. White is condemned by all the old
authorities, but a white chest and white toes, occurring as they
do in a great many of the darkest-coloured dogs, are not so
greatly objected to, but the less the better, as the Deerhound
is a self-coloured dog. A white blaze on the head, or a
white collar, should entirely disqualify. In other cases,
though passable, yet an attempt should be made to get rid
of white markings. The less white the better, but a slight
white tip to the stern occurs in the best strains.—*Height of
Dogs*—From 28 to 30 inches, or even more if there be
symmetry without coarseness, but which is rare.—*Height of
Bitches*—From 26 inches upwards. There can be no
objection to a bitch being large, unless too coarse, as even
at her greatest height she does not approach that of the
dog, and, therefore, could not have been too big for work,
as over-big dogs are. Besides, a big bitch is good for
breeding and keeping up the size.—*Weight*—From 85 to
105 lbs. in dogs ; from 65 to 80 lbs. in bitches.

There is but little doubt that the best specimens of
the breed have emanated from Scotland, as a glance at the
pedigrees of the present-day hounds will show. Sir John
McNeill, Lord Edward Bentinck, and the late Cameron of
Lochiel owned hounds which, in their day, could not be
beaten, either for sport or show. The late Edwin Weston
Bell owned a breed particularly his own ; but his stud,
in the writer's opinion, originated from the strains of
" Blackmount," " Chesthill," and " Donavourd." The name
of William Gow, who, happily, is still with us, and who

Photo. by J. Russell & Sons, London.

CH. ST. RONAN'S RHYME.

is one of our best judges, must not be omitted ; but beyond breeding a litter once a year he has taken no part in the pursuit of his hobby for the last fifteen years.

Of the dogs exhibited during the last twenty years, the foremost was Ch. Selwood Morven, bred by Mr. Hood Wright, and which was awarded the championship at every important show. He was a very big and massive hound, measuring 33 inches at the shoulder. Strange to say, he was never a success at stud, although used by the majority of kennels, both in Scotland and England. He was, however, bred from parents who, to the best of the writer's belief, never won a prize, namely, Selwood Hoolachan ex Selwood Flora. One of the most famous sires was Ch. Swift, a magnificent hound, and one of the pillars of the breed. Many of the best specimens of to-day claim this hound as one of their fore-fathers. Amongst other well known dogs he sired Ch. Selwood Dhouran, Ch. Kelso and Ch. Forester, the last-named being another very successful sire. Coming to a later period, we find Ch. Rufford Bend Or (a smaller hound, but certainly one of the most typical), Ch. Fingall, Ch. Earl II. and Ch. St. Ronan's Ranger. The last-named is probably the chief sire of the present day, amongst his progeny being Ch. St. Ronan's Rhyme, the most successful Deerhound (a bitch) ever exhibited. She has taken every cup and championship for which she has competed. In October, 1906, she was adjudged, at the Kennel Club Show, the best dog of all breeds in the Show; and the following week she repeated the same feat at Edinburgh. Ch. Talisman is another of Ranger's progeny. Amongst the best bitches are Ch. Callack, Ch. Braie, Ch. Bluebell, Ch. Craigie, and Ch. Avening May.

The interests of the breed are well attended to by the Deerhound Club, which provides many prizes and medals for competition at the principal shows.

The subject of breeding, generally, has already been dealt with (see page 305), and it is only necessary, here, to state that, in the writer's experience, the dam has the greater influence on the progeny.

The matter of feeding is also dealt with elsewhere. (*See* FOOD AND FEEDING). It should be remembered, however, that Deerhounds bred and reared in the South are not as a rule as hardy as those brought up in the North, and consequently require more dainty food. Amongst other foods which the writer has found suitable are biscuits, sheep and bullocks' heads (boiled), rice, fish and, above all, leeks, onions, etc.

The Deerhound requires plenty of exercise ; no specimen has ever been known to thrive or be in proper condition which has been housed in kennels and not given full liberty.

As regards preparing for show, some persons imagine that this can be done in a few days. Such is not the case. The writer has never met with any trouble in this connection, his rule being to keep his hounds in such a condition that they are ready for exhibition at all times.

In conclusion, the writer is well satisfied with the existing type. The hounds at the present time are, in his opinion, better than they have ever been—they are better in size, harder in coat, straighter in limb and stronger in body. The virtues of the grand old Watch Dog of Scotland cannot be praised too highly. That the breed may continue to improve and to advance in public esteem and favour is the earnest hope of the writer.

The following lines, taken from the Gaelic, aptly describe the Deerhound ; the writer regrets he is unable to give the name of the author :—

> *An eye of sloe, with ear not low,*
> *With horse's breast, with depth of chest,*
> *With breadth of loin and curve in groin*
> *And nape set far behind the head:*
> *Such were the dogs that Fingal bred.*

HARRY RAWSON.

CHAPTER VIII.

TRAINING THE DEER HOUND.

ON all things there is a main point, also certain rules which should never be forgotten in training hounds, especially the age and the way to train them. My experience has taught me that it is a big mistake to allow a young deer hound to go in the woods before he is 12 to 15 months old," says a Canadian hunter.

At a year old a hound should know how to lead well, that is not to pull on the chain for all he is worth ahead of his master but to follow behind him through every place he passes, if between, under or over logs as well as fences, to follow exactly the same trail as his master. A dog or a pair coupled together, so trained, can be easily led in any bush without any bother whatever. It is not at all necessary that a dog should lead in front of his master to find a trail. A dog with a keen nose can pick a trail from the air several yards before reaching it. He will then pull you in the direction of the same and if the scent is fresh, he will be anxious to follow it, then if the hunter is a man who understands his business, he will examine the track by following it 100 yards or so and if suitable and going (if it is a deer) in the right direction and if the wind is also right, will then allow his hound to go.

A dog which knows his business will not open the minute he gets the scent but will cover the ground fast and save his steam until he has jumped the deer or fox, then open his value and

The Deer Seeks Refuge in Deep Water.

if he is a flyer he will water more deer in five hours than another which gives tongue as soon as he takes the scent in five days for the reason that a dog which opens the very instant he finds a trail will have to cover 20 times more ground to bring his deer to water, than the one which does not.

A hound should not be gun or water shy but should be shy of strangers, traps and of poisoned baits. He should know how to swim across a river or lake and where to land. He should have but one master and obey him to the word and this without the use of the whip. He should know how to ride in a canoe. All this can be taught to him in about 3 months and he should know all these things before he is broken to hunt.

The next thing is to accustom your dog to the gun. This is easily done. All you have to do is to take your gun and dog into a field and once there to tie your dog say five or six feet from you, then to shoot the gun and after every shot to speak kindly to your dog and make him smell the gun. In a day or so repeat as before and the moment you see that your dog is not afraid let him loose and shoot again and always pet him. He will then know what a gun is. So when your young hound knows the gun, the canoe and water, he may be taught to be shy of strangers, traps and of poisoned baits.

To break a dog to hunt, you must not allow him to go in the bush whenever he likes. A dog that hunts without being in the company of his master will never be a well trained dog. Therefore, you must lead him in the bush and if you have a well trained dog, you may couple him with the young one and walk until you find a good trail then follow it with the dogs till you see that the young one has caught scent right, then let go the young hound first and the "old timer" last. If the hound comes from hunting stock, he will hang to the trail with the other dog and he will only turn up with him but for some reason or another, should the young hound come back to you, "don't get mad and kick or beat him." No, this is a great error and many are the dogs which have been spoiled that way. Instead of beating, speak kindly to him and pet him a few seconds and keep moving towards where the chase is going.

Don't excite your dog, pay no attention to him. If he wants to follow you at your heels, let him do so and once you reach a place where likely the other dog is going to pass, stay there and when the old dog comes along, the young one will again join and may stay this time with him, as the scent will be hot and the chances are ten to one that the young hound will take a hand in the music. But if after ten, or twenty minutes, he should again return, treat him as before. Be always kind to him. If you have no old dog to train your young one, go with your dog and show him the game you want him to hunt, lead him until you kill one, then blood him. The blooding is the "A, B, C" of training. Allow him to smell the game all he likes, speak kindly to him even if he bites the game, don't kick him off or use a stick on him, as I have often seen done by some fellows who pretend that to teach a hound you must abuse him. If you want a foolish dog, that is the way to use him but if you desire an intelligent one, you must encourage him.

After a dog has been well blooded (the blooding is done by rubbing the hot blood of the game on the front legs, as well as on the sides of the dog), you may turn him loose or you may lead him until you find another trail. He will at once be anxious to follow. Let him lead for a hundred yards and once you are sure that he has the scent in the right direction, let him go and if that hound comes from trained stock, he will run that scent immediately and should he only be away for five, ten or more minutes and come back to you, speak kindly to him and tell him to hunt. Always mention his name and keep moving in the direction where you suppose the game is.

It is a good thing that a young dog backs his own tracks at first, as it teaches him that he can find you when he likes and a hound that does this after each chase will never get lost no matter where you may go. In deer hunting, it has many advantages in so far, that when you are several miles from camp, after your dog has a start you keep moving and if you find where a deer has just passed, you can just sit there and wait for the return of the dog and as soon as he returns,

you just tie him and allow him to rest for fifteen
or twenty minutes and then you start him again.
I have often had two and sometimes four chases
in one forenoon and this without bother. Hounds
thus trained, will always return to camp every

Well Trained Hounds.

night for their feed and will be ready for the
next day.

Some hunters say that their dogs are so
good that when they turn them loose, they always stay away for three or four days and they
even go so far as to say, that they hunt night and
day during the whole time they are away. Well,

this is not the case at all. The reason is that they will chase a deer or fox for three or four hours or more and when they have watered the deer or holed their fox, will then start to ramble around and start after another and after watering their second deer, they will be so far away that they are unable to find their way back, and they will walk until they can go no more. They will then lie down for a long time and walk around and howl until they find somebody's trail, which they will follow to the end or until they land at a settler's house or at some shanty and will remain there.

Now how many dogs like these will a party of ten or twelve men require to hunt, during ten or fifteen days in a strange country? When a hound has been away three or four days, is he in condition to run the next day after his return? No, it will take him as many days to recover and often he will be of no use for the remainder of the hunt.

Dogs like these may suit men living in the country where there is game. Their dogs after having been lost several times will, through time, know the lay of the country and be fairly good dogs at home, but take these hounds in a strange country, of what use and how many will a hunting party require to hunt every day of their outing? Well, they will require a car-load and besides several men to hunt the dogs. Such dogs as these don't stay with me, as I consider them a nuisance, especially for city sportsmen, who are so busy during the whole year that they can only take a few weeks holiday every year, they require a strain of hounds on which they can depend every day of their hunt. I want a dog to be a flyer and to back track after every chase and to find me in the bush and not make for camp after his chase or wait at the shore until some "Johnny Sneakum" comes along with his canoe and says, "Get in Jack," and that Jack is only too glad to jump in and the next thing is that you don't see Jack for the balance of the season, but you will learn later on that Jack has been half starved that it will cost you $5.00 to $10.00 for the board if you desire to get Jack.

I will say here that I owe my life to two of my hounds. I was lost once in the woods in a blinding snow storm. This was in Western Ontario amongst a range of sappy pine hills. I was about five miles from camp. In the morning when I left the weather was very fine but it soon started to snow and the storm lasted until about 9 P. M. I was soaking wet and I had left my compass at camp, my matches were all wet and I slept in the bush. At 10 A. M. I had started my two hounds and about 11 A. M. they came back to me. It was just commencing to snow heavily but thinking it would not last long, I made for another hill where I was aware, if any deer started from there it was a sure run for our men, so I arrived there in due time and got a start. It was still snowing very heavily. I then pointed for home. I had about five miles more to reach our camp when I came to a place where a deer had just left his nest, so I thought that I could get a shot at him but after having followed him for about an hour, I gave him up and I tried to make for camp.

Well, instead of making for camp, I made a circle and came back to the same place where I had left the deer's track. It was 4 P. M., when my dogs came back to me. I knew then that I was completely turned so I decided to spend the night right there. I looked for a sheltered place and after removing all the snow I could I lay down with my back against a big flat stone and with my two dogs lying near me. We were quite comfortable and early in the morning, I pointed for camp. Now if these dogs had not returned to me, I really believe that I would not be able to write this, as their heat preserved me from freezing to death.

THE DEERHOUND

THE Deerhound is one of the most decorative of dogs, impressively stately and picturesque wherever he is seen, whether it be amid the surroundings of the baronial hall, reclining at luxurious length before the open hearth in the fitful light of the log fire that flickers on polished armour and tarnished tapestry ; out in the open, straining at the leash as he scents the dewy air, or gracefully bounding over the purple of his native hills. Grace and majesty are in his every movement and attitude, and even to the most prosaic mind there is about him the inseparable glamour of feudal romance and poetry. He is at his best alert in the excitement of the chase ; but all too rare now is the inspiring sight that once was common among the mountains of Morven and the glens of Argyll of the deep-voiced hound speeding in pursuit of his antlered prey, racing him at full stretch along the mountain's ridge, or baying him at last in the fastness of darksome corrie or deep ravine. Gone are the good romantic days of stalking beloved by Scrope. The Highlands have lost their loneliness, and the inventions of the modern gunsmith have robbed one of the grandest of hunting dogs of his glory, relegating him to the life of a pedestrian pet, whose highest dignity is the winning of a pecuniary prize under Kennel Club rules.

Historians of the Deerhound associate him with the original Irish Wolfdog, of whom he is obviously a close relative, and it is sure that when the wolf still lingered in the land it was the frequent quarry of the Highland as of the Hibernian hound. Legend has it that Prince Ossian, son of Fingal, King of Morven, hunted the wolf with the grey, long-bounding dogs.

" Swift-footed Luath " and " White-breasted Bran " are among the names of Ossian's hounds. I am disposed to affirm that the old Irish Wolfhound and the Highland Deerhound are not only intimately allied in form and nature, but that they are two strains of an identical breed, altered only in size by circumstance and environment.

Whatever the source of the Highland Deerhound, and at whatever period it became distinct from its now larger Irish relative, it was recognised as a native dog in Scotland in very early times, and it was distinguished as being superior in strength and beauty to the hounds of the Picts.

From remote days the Scottish nobles cherished their strains of Deerhound, seeking glorious sport in the Highland forests. The red deer belonged by inexorable law to the kings of Scotland, and great drives, which often lasted for several days, were made to round up the herds into given neighbourhoods for the pleasure of the court, as in the reign of Queen Mary. But the organised coursing of deer by courtiers ceased during the Stuart troubles, and was left in the hands of retainers, who thus replenished their chief's larder.

The revival of deerstalking dates back hardly further than a hundred years. It reached its greatest popularity in the Highlands at the time when the late Queen and Prince Albert were in residence at Balmoral. Solomon, Hector, and Bran were among the Balmoral hounds. Bran was an especially fine animal—one of the best of his time, standing over thirty inches in height.

Two historic feats of strength and endurance illustrate the tenacity of the Deerhound at work. A brace of half-bred dogs, named Percy and Douglas, the property of Mr. Scrope, kept a stag at bay from Saturday night to Monday morning ; and the pure bred Bran by himself pulled down two unwounded stags, one carrying ten and the other eleven tines. These, of course, are record performances, but they demonstrate the possibilities of the Deerhound when trained to his natural sport.

MRS. ARMSTRONG'S DEERHOUND CH. TALISMAN

Driving was commonly resorted to in the extensive forests, but nowadays when forests are sub-divided into limited shootings the deer are seldom moved from their home preserves, whilst with the use of improved telescopes and the small-bore rifle, stalking has gone out of fashion. With guns having a muzzle velocity of 2,500 feet per second, it is no longer necessary for sportsmen stealthily to stalk their game to come within easy range, and as for hounds, they have become a doubtful appendage to the chase.

Primarily and essentially the Deerhound belongs to the order *Agaseus*, hunting by sight and not by scent, and although he may indeed occasionally put his nose to the ground, yet his powers of scent are not remarkable. His vocation, therefore, has undergone a change, and it was recently ascertained that of sixty deer forests there were only six upon which Deerhounds were kept for sporting purposes.

Happily the Deerhound has suffered no decline in the favour bestowed upon him for his own sake. The contrary is rather the case, and he is still an aristocrat among dogs, valued for his good looks, the symmetry of his form, his grace and elegance, and even more so for his faithful and affectionate nature. Sir Walter Scott declared that he was " a most perfect creature of heaven," and when one sees him represented in so beautiful a specimen of his noble race as St. Ronan's Rhyme, for example, or Talisman, or Ayrshire, one is tempted to echo this high praise.

Seven-and-twenty years ago Captain Graham drew up a list of the most notable dogs of the last century. Among these were Sir St. George Gore's Gruim (1843-44), Black Bran (1850-51) ; the Marquis of Breadalbane's King of the Forest, said to stand 33 inches high ; Mr. Beaseley's Alder (1863-67), bred by Sir John McNeill of Colonsay ; Mr. Donald Cameron's Torrum (1869), and his two sons Monzie and Young Torrum ; and Mr. Dadley's Hector, who was probably the best-bred dog living in the early eighties. Torrum, however, appears to have been the most successful of these dogs at stud. He was an exceedingly grand specimen of his race, strong framed, with plenty of hair of a blue brindle colour. Captain Graham's own dog Keildar, who had been trained for deerstalking in Windsor Park, was perhaps one of the most elegant and aristocratic-looking Deerhounds ever seen. His full height was 30 inches, girth 33½ inches, and weight, 95 lbs., his colour bluish fawn, slightly brindled, the muzzle and ears being blue. His nearest competitor for perfection was, after Hector, probably Mr. Hood Wright's Bevis, a darkish red brown brindle of about 29 inches. Mr. Wright was the breeder of Champion Selwood Morven, who was the celebrity of his race about 1897, and who became the property of Mr. Harry Rawson. This stately dog was a dark heather brindle, standing 32½ inches at the shoulder, with a chest girth of 34½ inches.

A few years ago breeders were inclined to mar the beauty of the Deerhound by a too anxious endeavour to obtain great size rather than to preserve the genuine type ; but this error has been sufficiently corrected, with the result that symmetry and elegance conjoined with the desired attributes of speed are not sacrificed. The qualities aimed at now are a height of something less than 30 inches, and a weight not greater than 105 lbs., with straight fore-legs and short, cat-like feet, a deep chest, with broad, powerful loins, slightly arched, and strength of hind-quarters, with well-bent stifles, and the hocks well let down. Straight stifles are objectionable, giving a stilty appearance. Thick shoulders are equally a blemish to be avoided, as also a too great heaviness of bone. The following is the accepted standard of merit.

Head—The head should be broadest at the ears, tapering slightly to the eyes, with the muzzle tapering more decidedly to the nose. The muzzle should be pointed, but the teeth and lips level. The head should be long, the skull flat rather than round, with a very slight rise over the eyes, but with nothing approaching a stop. The skull should be coated with moderately long hair which is softer than the rest of the coat. The nose should be black (though in some blue-fawns the colour is blue) and slightly aquiline. In the lighter-coloured dogs a black muzzle is preferred. There should be a good moustache of rather silky hair, and a fair beard. **Ears**—The ears should be set on high, and, in repose, folded back like the Greyhound's, though raised above the head in excitement without losing the fold, and even, in some cases, semi-erect. A prick ear is bad. A big, thick ear, hanging flat to the head, or heavily coated with long hair, is the worst of faults. The ear should be soft, glossy, and like a mouse's coat to the touch, and the smaller it is the better. It should have no long coat or long fringe, but there is often a silky, silvery coat on the body of the ear and the tip. Whatever the general colour, the ears should be black or dark-coloured. **Neck and Shoulders**—The neck should be long—that is, of the length that befits the Greyhound character of the dog. An over-long neck is not necessary, nor desirable, for the dog is not required to stoop in his work like a Greyhound, and it must be remembered that the mane, which every good specimen should have, detracts from the apparent length of neck. Moreover, a Deerhound requires a very strong neck to hold a stag. The nape of the neck should be very prominent where the head is set on, and the throat should be clean-cut at the angle and prominent. The shoulders should be well sloped, the blades well back, with not too much width between them. Loaded and straight shoulders are very bad faults. **Stern**—Stern should be tolerably long, tapering, and reaching to within 1½ inches of the ground, and about 1½ inches below the hocks. When the dog is still, dropped perfectly straight down, or curved. When in motion it should be curved when excited, in no case to be lifted out of the line of the back. It should be well covered with hair, on the inside thick and wiry, under-side longer, and towards the end a slight fringe is not objectionable. A curl or ring tail is very undesirable. **Eyes**—The eyes should be dark : generally they are dark brown or hazel. A very light eye is not liked. The eye is moderately full with a soft look in repose, but a keen, far-away gaze when the dog is roused. The rims of the eyelids should be black. **Body**—The body and general formation is that of a Greyhound of larger size and bone. Chest deep rather than broad, but not too narrow and flat-sided. The loin well arched and drooping to the tail. A straight back is not desirable, this formation being unsuitable for going uphill, and very unsightly. **Legs and Feet**—The legs should be broad and flat, a good broad forearm and elbow being desirable. Fore-legs, of course, as straight as possible. Feet close and compact, with well-arched toes. The hind-quarters drooping, and as broad and powerful as possible, the hips being set wide apart. The hind-legs should be well bent at the stifle, with great length from the hip to the hock, which should be broad and flat. Cow hocks, weak pasterns, straight stifles, and splay feet are very bad faults. **Coat**—The hair on the body, neck, and quarters should be harsh and wiry, and about 3 inches or 4 inches long ; that on the head, breast, and belly is much softer. There should be a slight hairy fringe on the inside of the fore and hind-legs, but nothing approaching to the feathering of a Collie. The Deerhound should be a shaggy dog, but not over coated. A woolly coat is bad. Some good strains have a slight mixture of silky coat with the hard, which is preferable to a woolly coat, but the proper covering is a thick, close-lying, ragged coat, harsh or crisp to the touch. **Colour**—Colour is much a matter of fancy. But there is no manner of doubt that the dark blue-grey is the most preferred. Next come the darker and lighter greys or brindles, the darkest being generally preferred. Yellow and sandy-red or red-fawn, especially with black points—*i.e.*, ears and muzzle—are also in equal estimation, this being the colour of the oldest known strains, the McNeil and the Chesthill Menzies. White is condemned by all the old authorities, but a white chest and white toes, occurring as they do in a great many of the darkest-coloured dogs, are not so greatly objected to, but the less the better, as the Deerhound is a self-coloured dog. A white blaze on the head or a white collar should entirely disqualify. In other cases, though passable, an attempt should be made to get rid of white markings. The less white the better, but a slight white tip to the stern occurs in the best strains. **Height of Dogs**—From 28 inches to 30 inches, or even more if there be symmetry without coarseness, which, however, is rare. **Height of Bitches**—From 26 inches upwards. There can be no objection to a bitch being large, unless she is too coarse, as even at her greatest height she does not approach that of the dog, and, therefore, could not well be too big for work, as over-big dogs are. Besides, a big bitch is good for breeding and keeping up the size. **Weight**—From 85 pounds to 105 pounds in dogs ; from 65 pounds to 80 pounds in bitches.

Among the more prominent owners of Deerhounds at the present time are Mrs. H. Armstrong, Mrs. W. C. Grew, Mrs. Janvrin Dickson, Miss A. Doxford, Mr. Harry Rawson, and Mr. H. McLauchin. Mrs. Armstrong is the breeder of two beautiful dog hounds in Talisman and Laird of Abbotsford, and of· two typically good bitches in Fair Maid of Perth and Bride of Lammermoor. Mrs. Grew owns many admirable specimens, among them being Blair Athol, Ayrshire, Kenilworth, and Ferraline. Her Ayrshire is considered by some judges to be the most perfect Deerhound exhibited for some time past. He is somewhat large, perhaps, but he is throughout a hound of excellent quality and character, having a most typical head, with lovely eyes and expression, perfect front, feet and hind-quarters. Other judges would give the palm to Mr. Harry Rawson's St. Ronan's Ranger, who is certainly difficult to excel in all the characteristics most desirable in the breed.

This variety of hound is built upon similar lines to that of the Irish Wolfhound, the Greyhound, and Borzoi or Russian Wolfhound, but when compared to the Greyhound the Deerhound is obviously a much heavier type of dog, and capable of undergoing a more severe form of work, as hunting the deer in mountainous districts constituted the work for which the breed was originally designed. At the present time Deerhounds are more kept for companionship than aught else, and being extremely handsome dogs, of a quiet, sociable temperament, readily lend themselves for such a purpose. They are of hardy constitution, and young stock is not particularly difficult to rear, but anyone contemplating founding a kennel of these hounds ought to have plenty of room at his disposal, as the puppies require almost unlimited exercise, otherwise various faults are liable to develop. The term Staghound and Deerhound must not be accepted as synonymous, some Deerhounds being used for hunting the stag and designated Staghounds,

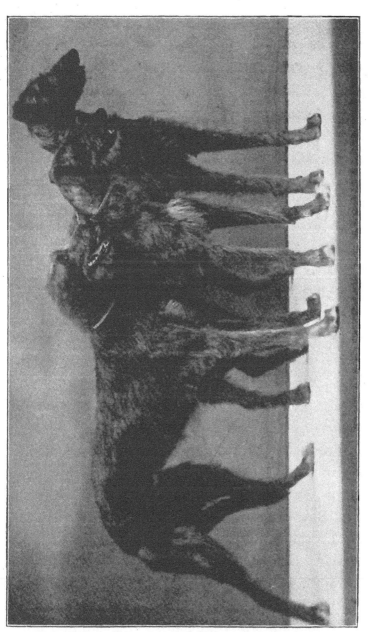

A TRIO OF DEERHOUNDS

To face page 164

HOUNDS

whilst many Foxhounds are used for the same purpose and consequently are also referred to as Staghounds. Concerning the origin of the Scottish Deerhound there is very little reliable information for one's guidance, nevertheless there is good grounds for believing that the breed is an ancient one, as shown by some of the older records of Scottish sport.

The reason why the Irish Wolfhound should be regarded as the progenitor of the Deerhound is a dictum no more tenable than the converse, excluding of course the supposed greater antiquity of the former.

Certain breeders of Deerhounds have adopted the plan of an out-cross such as the Russian Wolfhound, the Irish Wolfhound, also the Greyhound, with, in some instances, satisfactory results. But this variety of hound is not one that has suffered much through prolonged inter-breeding, and it is very questionable whether any permanent good follows the introduction of an alien cross.

Deerhounds vary in their colour; brindle either light or dark, reddish yellow or reddish fawn and dark blue with a shade of grey are the usual colours. Some Deerhounds have black points confined to the ears and muzzle, whereas others have white about the head or neck, chest or toes; but the presence of white in any of these situations is distinctly objectionable, although a few white hairs at the end of a tail are of no importance, and very little more so when upon the breast. Nevertheless, white hair is certainly an indication that other than Deerhound blood has been introduced, it may be generations since. A light brindle with dark brindle shadings, likewise a bluish-grey, are colours highly esteemed, though colour is secondary to a good all-round conformation.

As in most other hound-breeding, there is a tendency to breed hounds either too big or too small, the medium-sized hound being the most useful when it comes to an analysis of the working dog. If a Deerhound is too cumbersome it is lacking in speed and agility. The coat should be rather wiry in texture and about three inches in length along the upper border of the neck, withers and back, but it is softer and shorter on the under part of the body; density of coat is as important as crispness of it; any tendency towards woolliness is objectionable.

The weight for dogs ranges from 80 to 110 lbs., and for bitches from 60 to 90 lbs.; whilst the average height for dogs ought to be 29 or 30 in., bitches being a trifle less. It seems almost needless to state that a Deerhound must have plenty of chest capacity, so that a deep chest but not a wide breast is the correct conformation. The more room for the free play of heart and lungs the greater the endurance. The back and the loins must be strong, the latter

DEERHOUND

well arched, this form of conformation being regarded as the most suitable for work in mountainous localities. Three important essentials are bone, muscle and substance, and any tendency to lightness of bone, want of muscular development or weakness of joints must be looked upon with disfavour. As in most other varieties of hounds, excepting the short-legged breeds, " cow-hocks " and " splay " feet are common defects, nevertheless irremediable. The forearm should be broad in all proportions, of goodly length and big at the elbow and pastern joints; fine shoulders and strong first and second thighs, together with a long tapering stern, slightly curved but hanging below the level of the hocks, are necessary points of beauty. The head should be long, broad in the muzzle, but showing no evidence of indentation or " stop." The hair on the skull is softer than that on the body, and in light-coloured dogs a black muzzle materially adds to the appearance of the animal. The nostrils should be black, the ears set on high and, when dog is at repose, folded back, but under excitement raised; the softer and finer the texture of the ear the better. Dark brown or hazel-coloured eyes are the correct type in the Deer-hound.

THE DEERHOUND

James I and Queen Anne were out shooting, the Queen shot the King's favourite Deerhound. 'At which the King stormed exceedingly awhile,' but hearing who was responsible 'wished her not to be troubled with it, for he should love her none the worse.'

Bred from Irish Wolfhounds and Greyhounds, this dog is the very embodiment of graceful strength ; a very ancient breed, full of sterling characters. *Deirhoundis*, 1528.

It weighs about 100 lb, and stands 30 to 32 inches at the shoulder. A huge, heavily-built, rough-haired greyhound, with a rough, hard, strong coat, varying in colour from blue to wheatons and brindles. Heavily built, but graceful.

In their souls is the art of killing ; and deer cause mad excitement, even when seen for the first time. How to kill is instinctive. They race after their quarry ; there is no attempt to seize the hind legs, but the neck is seized, pulled down, the deer's head strikes the ground, breaks its own neck. Care should be taken to prevent by lack of skill in breeding, loss of type, weak heads and lack of the racy style, characteristic of the real thing.

'An eye of a sloe,
An ear not low,
A horse's breast,
And deep in chest,
And broad in loin,
And strong in groin,
With nape set far behind the head,
Such were the dogs that Fingal bred.'

THE DEERHOUND

Deerhounds are a variety of Greyhound, and are probably closely related to the one time numerous rough-haired Greyhound of Yorkshire. The Deerhound is often mistaken for the Irish Wolfhound, and *vice versa*, but the Deerhound is lithely, delicately built, when compared with the Irish Wolfhound, a massive dog. Further, the head of the Deerhound is of Greyhound type, whilst that of the Irish Wolfhound is of Great Dane type. The Deerhound breed is of considerable antiquity. It is claimed that the breed is mentioned in Hector Boethius' *Pitscottie's History* as *Deirhoundis*, but this is not so. Boethius certainly mentions three varieties of Scottish dogs to be of marvellous nature, one of which is " hardy and swift," and may possibly be the Scottish Deerhound. But the constantly repeated assertion that in that book it is stated that various lords brought their " Deirhoundis " with them is a statement made by Dalziel in all good faith, and ever afterwards copied. Dalziel was misled, so were all other authors. Pitscottie's work was first published in 1575. It came out in various editions, but never is the word *Deirhoundis*, or other form of this word, used. The explanation is that 153 years later, in 1728, a man by name of Linsay wrote a book which Dr. Johnson, I believe, described as the work of a knave.[1] The book, on the title page, is stated to be a History of Scotland and Robert Linsay to be " of Pitscottie." In this book the word *Deirhoundis* is *not* used, but the word *Hounds*. Nearly a hundred years later, in 1814, a new edition of Linsay's book was printed, and, presumably, to give an appearance of an early work of historical importance, those responsible **altered the text** and put the word *Deirhoundis* in place of Mr. Linsay's *Hounds* ! Dalziel mistook the 1814 book to be a copy of the original Pitscottie of 1575, and everybody, as I have already stated, relied on Dalziel, and were consequently misled ! There is, however, evidence, though not of a very reliable nature, that the Deerhound was kept in Scotland about that time, for in a 1577 edition of the genuine *Pitscottie's History of Scotland* a crude woodcut of three huntsmen shows, with them, a large dog of Greyhound type.[2] I have made a rough calculation and certain measurements, and have come to the conclusion that if my calculations are correct this dog stood at least 33 inches at the shoulder. The modern Deerhound stands from 28 to 30 inches (bitches 26 inches upwards). Whether the dog was smooth-haired or rough-haired is difficult to say, for although the woodcut shows an unevenness on the tail, it may not necessarily represent a rough coat, nor does it follow that the shading on the body suggests a coat of that kind. In 1583, in a book of Animals, a large rough-haired Greyhound is depicted,[3] and in 1637 a dog of the Deerhound type appears in the work of Aldrovandus, who names it the *White-Hairy Greyhound*,[4] but although Aldrovandus quotes the original Pitscottie, including the passage referred to (the three Scottish dogs of a marvellous nature), in his text he makes no suggestion that the White-Hairy Greyhound (as one might hope he would) is one of these Scottish dogs.

The first evidence of a Deerhound occurs (except the Irish Greyhound note made by the Pennyless Pilgrim, *His Majesty's Water Pot*, in 1620, which I allude to in the section on Irish Wolfhounds) in 1769, when Pennant, the English naturalist and antiquarian, visited Gordon Castle and saw what he describes as " the true Highland Greyhound," a large dog covered with long hair. He tells us that this dog had been greatly kept by the

Scottish chiefs and used in the " stag chases," and that it had become very scarce. In 1838 Scrope deals with the breed in his book, *The Art of Deer-stalking*.

The Deerhound had been developed for strength and speed. They were used to overtake wounded stags and hold them at bay. They were also used to course stags in the open country. With the improvement of the rifle the Deerhound was no longer so much required. Stags, when shot, were too badly wounded to go far. The Deerhound lost the patronage of the owners of deer-forests, and there seemed reason to believe that the breed would die out completely. Probably due to Scrope's book and the excellent illustrations it contained, the interest in the breed returned, and by 1842 the Deerhound was commonly kept in Scotland, and could claim to be a national breed. Of the important owners of that time were the family of the Menzies of Chesthill, Loch Tay, who had a noted pure strain.[1] The Macneile's of Colonsay were also well known for their dogs. The resemblance between the rough-haired Greyhound of Yorkshire and the Deerhound of Scotland was by no means pleasing, and *Stonehenge* (Walsh) gives us this delightfully naïve information, that there were, indeed, two different breeds, the Scottish Deerhound and rough Greyhound, identical in appearance, but *readily distinguished by the way they ran and the way they played* ! In the next few years the breed became much in fashion, for at Sandringham Her Majesty Queen Victoria had Deerhounds in her kennels, under the care of a Mr. Cole. Many dogs later were known as the *Mr. Cole Breed*. The breed had lost size, and there were many not more than 26 inches high, though now and again an outstanding specimen was to be met with, such as Lord Breadalbane's *King of the Forest*, which stood 33 inches high. Attempts were made to bring the breed back to its former excellence by introducing other breeds,[2] including the Borzoi. Such, indeed, was *Keildar*, a brindle fawn, standing 30¼ inches high, with a soft but not woolly coat, which Captain Graham purchased from Mr. Cole's widow on February 15, 1870. Her grandmother was a " black Russian Wolfhound," and on her grandfather's side she went back to a pure bred Deerhound dog named *Tank*, brought from Tankerville Castle by Cole about the year 1858. The Deerhound breed has greatly to thank Captain Graham, who started a kennel of Deerhounds on his return from India, entirely in order to rebuild the Irish Wolfhound. The first he had was *Ella*, born in May, 1860. She was bred by Colonel Inge. She was 25½ inches high, with ears and head pale yellow, though her body was more sandy in colour. She came from a Macpherson dog, bred by Macpherson of Ruthven. Deerhounds were then of many types, some had wonderful hard coats, others had coats like sheep—so woolly. Some were well built, some full of quality, some just as coarse. Ch. *Old Torrom*, born in the autumn of 1866, had, when adult, a very bad coat and bad limbs, and a very coarse head and big ears, described as " all over of the coarsest." He went back to *King of the Forest*. We read that Lord Breadalbane's *Paddy*, born in the autumn of 1876, was " purchased by a Mr. Gant (a pupil of the Chaplain at Taymouth Castle), and was left at Taymouth when Mr. Gant went to Australia." Such is a note on the pedigree of this dog, described as of good size, silver-grey in colour, with a good wiry coat. What charming names appear in these early pedigrees : *Bonnie Lass, Deene, Delio, Elshie, Heather Jock, Tarvie, Rossie Bruar, Rory Toseach, Croona.*

In 1892 the Deerhound Club was formed, and Mr. G. W. Hickman and

[1] This is to-day known as the *Monzie* strain.
[2] The Bloodhound was used in the pedigree of a dog named *Spey*, born in 1868.

Mr. R. Hood-Wright assisted by others drew out the standard description. With the formation of the Club and the registration of the dogs, outside crosses came to an end. This was not at the time to the breed's advantage, for it had by no means fully recovered. In 1895 the famous kennel of the Duke of Richmond and Gordon was dispersed in London, and the dogs, full of the lore of the forests, were sold at an average price of one guinea, the highest price paid six guineas ! In the years that followed the breed just held its own. In 1898 *Selwood Callack* was considered one of the best dogs living, but from his photograph he is seen to have poor hindquarters. There are many stories of dogs claimed to have been of that breed. It happened, so we learn, in the days of Bruce, that a white deer escaped the hounds of the King on each occasion. *Help* and *Hold* were two hounds of Sir William St. Clair, and he said that they would take the deer. The King offered the Forest of Pentland Moor to the head of Sir William, that the deer would reach the other side of March Burn, in spite of *Help* and *Hold*. The white deer, roused, reached the burn and plunged into the water. A few more yards, and she would have gained the other side. But *Help* and *Hold* bayed her, attacked, and held her, so that Sir William saved his head and obtained the broad acres of Pentland Moor. He rests now below a canopy of stone in Rosslyn Chapel, a Deerhound at his feet, so the story goes, but at the feet of the effigy is indeed a strange thing, bearing no resemblance to any breed of dog we know.

There is also the story how a Lord Tankerville purchased from a poacher a Deerhound, one that had never missed a deer. The poacher lived some seventy miles away. The dog, *Bran* by name, was placed in an enclosure, high palisades surrounded him. His late master, the poacher, went homeward filled with misgivings. But on nearing his cottage, who should come rushing out but *Bran* to welcome him ! There were only two ways home, one by the road his master travelled ; the other by swimming Loch Ericht, and it is presumed that *Bran* chose the latter way (which was by far the nearest) to return to the home he loved. The Loch is 14 miles long. For modern Deerhounds, see Plate 39 (18) and (40).

THE DEERHOUND.

The **head** is broadest at the ears, tapering slightly to the eyes, with the muzzle tapering more decidedly to the nose. The muzzle is pointed, but the teeth and lips level. The head is long, the skull flat rather than round, with a very slight rise over the eyes, but with nothing approaching a stop. The skull is coated with moderately long hair, which is softer than the rest of the coat. The nose is black (though in some blue-fawns the colour is blue) and slightly aquiline. In the lighter-coloured dogs a black muzzle is preferred. There is a good moustache of rather silky hair, and a fair beard. The **ears** are set on high and, in repose, folded back like the Greyhound's, though raised above the head in excitement without losing the fold, and even in some cases semi-erect. A prick ear is bad. A big thick ear hanging flat to the head or heavily coated with long hair is the worst of faults. The ear is soft, glossy and like a mouse's coat to the touch, and the smaller it is the better. It should have no long coat or long fringe, but there is often a silky, silvery coat on the body of the ear and the tip. Whatever the general colour, the ears black or dark-coloured. The **neck** is long—that is, of the length that befits the greyhound character of the dog. An over-long neck is not desirable. The **mane** makes the neck look shorter. The **nape** of the neck is very prominent where the head is set on, and the throat is clean cut at the angle and prominent. The **shoulders** are well sloped, the blades well back and not too much width between them. Loaded and straight shoulders are very bad faults. **Tail** should be reasonably long, tapering and reaching to within about 1½ inches off the ground. When the dog is still, dropped perfectly straight down, or curved. When the dog is in motion or excited the tail is curved. In no case to be lifted out of the line of the back. It is well covered with hair, on the inside, thick and wiry, underside longer, and towards the end a slight fringe is not objectionable. A curl or ring tail most undesirable. The **eyes** are dark ; generally dark brown or hazel. A very light eye is not liked. The eye is moderately full, with a soft look in repose, but a keen, far-away look when the dog is roused. The rims of the eyelids are black. The **body** and general formation is that of a greyhound of larger size and bone. Chest deep rather than broad, but not too narrow and flat-sided. The loin well arched and drooping to the tail. A straight back is not desirable. The **legs** are broad and flat—good broad forearm and elbow being desirable. Forelegs, as straight as possible. Feet close and compact, with well-arranged toes. The hindquarters drooping and broad and powerful, the hips set wide apart. The hind legs well bent at the stifle, with great length from the hip to the hock, which is broad and flat. Cow hocks, weak pasterns, straight stifles, and splay feet very bad faults. The **hair** on the body, neck and quarters is harsh and wiry, and about three or four inches long ; that on the head, breast and belly is much softer. There is a slight hairy fringe on the inside of the fore and hind legs, but nothing approaching the " feather " of a Colley. The Deerhound is a shaggy dog, but not over-coated. A woolly coat is bad. Some good strains have a mixture of silky coat with the hard, which is preferable to a woolly coat ; but the proper coat is a thick, close-lying, ragged coat, harsh or crisp to the touch. **Colour** is a matter of fancy. The dark blue-grey is the most preferred. Next comes the darker and lighter greys or brindles, the darkest being generally preferred. Yellow and sandy red or red-fawn, especially with black points, i.e., ears and muzzles are also in equal estimation, this being the colour of the oldest known strains, the M'Neil and Chesthill Menzies. White is condemned by all the old authorities, but a white chest and white toes, occurring as they do in a great many of the darkest-coloured dogs, are not so greatly objected to, but the less the better, as the Deerhound is a self-coloured dog. A white blaze on the head, or a white collar, should entirely disqualify. In other cases, though passable, yet an attempt should be made to get rid of white markings. The less white the better, but a slight white tip to the stern occurs in the best strains. **Height of dogs :** From 30 inches. **Height of bitches :** From 28 inches upwards. There can be no objection to a bitch being large, unless too coarse. **Weight :** Dogs from 85 lb. to 105 lb. ; bitches, from 65 lb. to 80 lb.

118

THE DEERHOUND

Origin and History.—Few dogs are more graceful for their size or more pleasing in appearance than the deerhound, and those of us who speculate upon the motives that determine fashion in these matters may well wonder how it is that the breed is not more widely distributed. One would have thought that those who like imposing proportions allied with gentleness of demeanour in their companions would have given attention to these handsome dogs. It is unusual, however, to meet one outside exhibition kennels and those are not as numerous as we would wish. Of later years, however, exhibitors have increased somewhat and an upward movement is perceptible, which it is to be hoped will continue to develop.

I can well believe, as I am told, that they make charming companions. The modern dog has his critics, some insisting that the craze for size has spoilt his characteristics. This is a story that we have heard since the end of last century, when some breeders advocated a smaller dog in the belief that it would afford a greater contrast to Irish wolfhounds. Of course, it is a fairly arguable proposition that a dog of medium size would be better fitted for coursing deer or tracking the wounded animal, but that is a matter that can only be determined after long experience. It is certain that some of the deerhounds of the early show days were as big as those we now know. A dog called *Black Bran* measured 31 inches at the shoulder and was 33½ inches round the chest. Sir George S. Gore's *Gruim* is said to have been between 32 and 33 inches in height. *Ch. Chieftain,* a son of *Ch. Bevis* and *Ch. Heather,* was nearly 32 inches and weighed over 100 lb. In America he was unbeaten, and through his son, *Buscar II,* his blood survives in much of the modern stock. *Buscar* was going about 1885. If anything is to be said in detraction of the present generation, it might be that the girth is less in proportion to the height than it was in the older dogs, which is a very important point when we are considering the question of stamina. Those who have the opportunity of reading the late Mr. George Cupples' "Scotch Deerhounds and their Masters," will find that in the early years of last century great size was much esteemed in the genuine working dogs, some of which measured 34 inches. Macdonell of Glengarry had several 36 inch dogs at Invergarry House.

Everyone is agreed that the deerhound belongs to a very old breed. Though the credibility of MacPherson's " Ossian " is in doubt, it is to be presumed that much of this long poem was derived from traditional sources, and we assume that his references to Fingal's dogs were justified. These dogs might have been either Irish Wolfhounds or deerhounds, but the probability is that they were the latter. Scott introduced them into several of his novels, sometimes calling them deer-greyhounds, and in the " Fortunes of Nigel " he makes his hero witness a course by "two tall greyhounds of the breed still used by the hardy deer-stalkers of the Scottish Highlands but which has been long unknown in England." They were closely followed by King James I, who cheered them on with " Weel dune, Bash—weel dune, Batty."

In an account of a visit to Scott at Abbotsford in 1830, J. E. Shortreed relates that the great novelist was almost constantly attended by three or four dogs : two large fellows, one a deerhound (a noble creature), the other a rough greyhound. Then there is the vivid description of the Knight of Gilsland's deerhound in " The Talisman " :

> " A most perfect creature of heaven ; of the old North breed—deep in the chest, strong in the stern, black colour and brindled on the breast and legs, · not spotted with white but just shaded into grey—strength to pull down a bull, swiftness to cote an antelope."

Centuries ago, the kings of Scotland and lesser chieftains were in the habit of summoning their clansmen to assemble with their hounds for mighty hunts, and reading of these gatherings one is almost forced to the conclusion that MacPherson was not greatly exceeding the bounds of poetic licence when he or Ossian wrote " a thousand dogs fly off at once, grey-bounding through the heath." After the rising of '45, which made it advisable for many of the noble families to fly to the Continent, the deerhounds seem to have become distributed among the commoner people. When Dr. Johnson visited the Isle of Skye, he saw " a race of brindled greyhounds, larger and stronger than those with which we course hares."

In more recent times, Queen Victoria and the Prince Consort were much attached to these dogs, of which they had a number at Windsor. *Keildar*, who came from the strain of McKenzie of Applecross, was used in Windsor Park for deer-stalking. Four of her Majesty's deerhounds were exhibited at a show at Islington in 1869. *Keildar* was at the show at the Crystal Palace in 1872, being then owned by Mr. H. Luckie, who entered him in the catalogue as " Age 8 years. Breeder, the

121

DEERHOUND : Champion *Padraic of Ross*, the property of the Misses Loughrey of Rosslyn, Londonderry, Ireland.

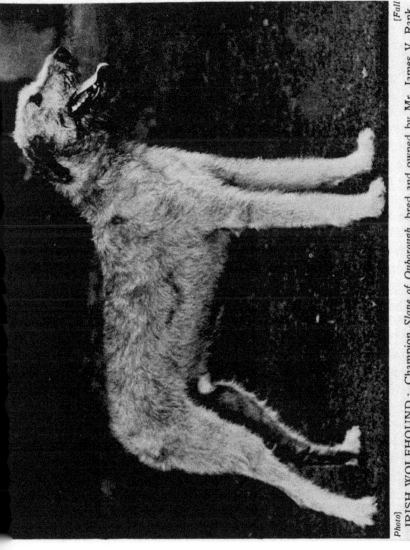

IRISH WOLFHOUND : Champion *Slane of Ouborough*, bred and owned by Mr. James V. Rank, of Ouborough, Godstone, Surrey.

123

late Mr. Cole, Head Keeper, Windsor Park. By *Oscar* (1st prize Islington, 1863)—*Hilda* (1st prize Cremorne, 1864). *Oscar* of McKingie's (of Applecross) breed. *Hilda* by *Old Keildar—Tank*, by the late Prince Consort's *Hector*."

I fancy that few breeds have retained their type throughout the show period more commendably than the deerhound, although it must be admitted that McNeil's *Buscar*, as painted by Landseer and exhibited in 1839, carries far less coat than we now expect to see.

Standard Description.—The Deerhound Club, of which the hon. secretaries are the Misses Loughrey, Rosslyn, Londonderry, is responsible for the accepted standard description. **Head.**— The head should be broadest at the ears, tapering slightly to the eyes with the muzzle tapering more decidedly to the nose. The muzzle should be pointed, the head long, the skull flat rather than round, with a very slight rise over the eyes but with nothing approaching a stop. There should be a good moustache of rather silky hair and a fair beard. The ears are set on high, folded back like the greyhound's in repose, though raised in excitement without losing the fold. The eyes are usually dark brown or hazel. A light eye is most undesirable. **Body.**—The body formation is that of a grey-hound on a larger scale. The neck should be long as befits a dog of the greyhound character, and the nape should be prominent where the head is set on. The shoulders should be well sloped and not loaded or straight. The chest is deep rather than broad, but not too narrow and flat-sided ; the loin is well arched and drooping to the tail. **Legs and Feet.**— The legs should be broad and flat, and the forelegs, of course, as straight as possible ; feet close and compact : hindquarters drooping and as broad and powerful as possible, the hips being wide apart. The hind legs should be well bent at the stifle with great length from hip to hock. Cow hocks, weak pasterns, straight stifles and splay feet are condemned. **Tail.**—Tail of tolerable length, tapers and reaches to within an inch and a half of the ground. When the dog is excited, it should be curved but not lifted out of the line of the back. A ring stern is very much disliked. *Coat.*—The hair on the body, neck and quarters should be harsh and wiry, about three or four inches long ; that on the head, breast and belly is much softer. There should be a slight hairy fringe on the inside of the legs, but nothing approaching the feather of a collie. A woolly coat is bad. *Colour.*—The subdued colouring always seems to me to fit in particularly well with the Scottish landscape. A dark blue-grey is most preferred, after which we have the darker and lighter greys or brindles, the darkest being generally liked. Yellow and sandy-red or red-fawn, especially with black points, are held in equal esteem ; the less white the better, though white on the chest and toes is not so greatly objected to, whereas a white blaze on the head or a white collar should entirely disqualify. **Height and Weight.**—The height of dogs may be from 30 inches or even more if there be symmetry without coarseness ; bitches should be some two inches less. The weight of dogs should be from 85 to 105 lb. ; that of bitches from 65 to 80 lb.

DEERHOUND : Champion *Padraic of Ross*, the property of the Misses Loughrey of Rosslyn, Londonderry, Ireland.

THE DEERHOUND

WITH most breeds of dogs we find a diversity of opinion as to their
true origin. With definite proof always absent, however, with some
breeds we are justified in taking a lot for granted, as we find certain
characteristics which enable us to justify our opinion as to the present-
day dogs, and from what breeds they have been produced.

To a certain extent a Scotch mist hangs over the deerhound's origin,
yet it is generally admitted that at some time or other the greyhound
was used as a cross, and many points are to be found that substantiate
this; then, again, the Irish wolfhound was used in order to obtain or
improve their rough coats.

The Deerhound is one of the hardiest of dogs bred, and is claimed
to be a true Hibernian breed. History tells us that the Scottish nobles

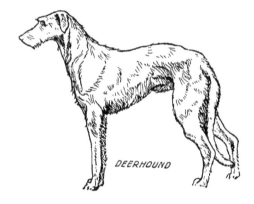

DEERHOUND

made use of them for sport in the Highland forests, and used their
dogs for hunting the red deer. Their great drives often lasted many
days, the deer being rounded up into certain neighbourhoods, and it
was not until the Stuart troubles that the organised coursing of deer
ceased.

Sir Walter Scott did much to create public interest in the breed,
and kept a large kennel of these hounds at Abbotsford; he also often
referred to their characteristics in his writings, while Sir Edwin Landseer's picture of a brace of Sir Walter Scott's well-known hounds has
done much to keep the breed before the public eye.

At the end of the eighteenth century, owing to the disappearance
of the boar and wolf, hunting gradually ceased in Scotland, and the

breed rapidly declined in size and number; but when deer-stalking reached its zenith about 100 years ago, they again became a popular hound, and were trained to course the deer in two ways, one being without the aid of man, while for the other they were trained to hold their prey at bay.

A hound of superior speed and courage was required in the former case, and speed was a great asset, as immediately the herd were in sight the hounds were slipped and the race began. On the rough ground the harder-footed deer held them off, but the dogs could quickly overtake their quarry on the flat, and would keep up the chase until they were within seizing distance, when they would usually spring at the leg so as to encumber the stag, until they had the opportunity of leaping at the throat.

When a stag stood at bay, it went badly for the dog if he made a frontal attack, as he would often have to give his life for his valour; but this breed of hound is so intelligent, it would await its opportunity so as to attack from behind, which resulted in the hound being unharmed and its prey always being killed.

Deerhounds provide excellent coursing both on the brown and white hill-hare, and are now used in increased numbers. The white hill-hare takes a good deal of killing among rocks and steep hills, but the Deerhound is a surefooted animal and seldom falls; hence he can traverse ground that a greyhound would get smashed up on.

They should have a long head, pointed muzzle, with teeth and lips level. The nose should be black, but in blue fawns it is sometimes blue; body formation that of a greyhound, but not too long, as they are not bred to do the same amount of stooping. The chest should be deep; loin well arched and drooping to the tail. Straight backs are a fault. The colour is a matter of fancy, but dark blue-grey is preferred. Deerhounds should carry a shaggy coat, but not overcoated. Woolly coats are bad.

Deerhounds.—The special attraction of the Scottish Deerhound may best be described as one of "atmosphere", for there is a glamour about him that seems to be peculiarly his own.

A NOTED KENNEL. [*Ralph Robinson.*

A charming study of Miss M. Richmond's Deerhounds. The resemblance to Irish Wolfhounds can here be seen. Of course, the Deerhound is much less powerful in build.

THE AUSTRIAN DEERHOUND.

Whilst the Deerhound in English-speaking countries means a Wire-haired large Greyhound, in Central Europe various types are known as Deerhounds, as the above Austrian dog suggests.

The worthy descendant of a noble ancestry, no other dog awakes a vision of armoured knights and ancient tapestried halls as does the Deerhound, whose characteristic far-away expression seems to recall the days of chivalry. His rugged, yet graceful exterior, his air of breeding, and his size, create an impression of beauty which accords well with his romantic history, and many artists have delighted to immortalize him in settings well suited to his picturesque appearance.

A long-established and thriving breed is known to have existed in Scotland—as elsewhere—prior to A.D. 1526. It refuses flatly, however, to emerge from the mists of obscurity prior to this date.

That the Deerhound is the Rough-coated Greyhound common to the British Isles from a very early age, we know, and Greyhounds, both Rough and Smooth, are mentioned by Arrian and others among the earliest authorities. Doctor Caius, in his book of *Englische Dogges*, A.D. 1576, speaking of Greyhounds, says· "Some are of a greater sorte and some of a lesser. Some are smoothe skynned and some are curled, the bigger therefor are appointed to hunt the bigger

beastes," and he specifies these "beastes" as "the buck, the harte, and the doe". Holinshed (A.D. 1577) corroborates this description, but uses "Shagg haired" instead of "curled", which presents a more comforting picture to the mind of the Deerhound-lover of to-day.

Endless instances occur about this date of the use of Rough Greyhounds, and it is perhaps interesting to note that the term "Greyhound" itself has long been a bone of contention among etymologists. Caius held that colour was not indicated by a derivation from "gre" or "grie", but a distinction, denoting the high rank these hounds occupied among their fellows. He says: "The Greyhound has his name of this word 'gre'. which word soundeth 'gradus' in Latin, in Englishe 'degree', because among all dogges these are the most principall. . . ." This opinion is borne out by other writers, and is a tenable theory. Gesner (A.D. 1560) uses the name Grewhound, and up to forty years ago Greyhounds in the south of Scotland were commonly called Grews. It is here worthy of note that the actual word Deerhound does not appear in old writings, and upon the one instance where "deirhoundis" is introduced (*Pitscottie's History of Scotland*, first published about A.D. 1600) proof exists that this was not in accord with the original edition.

The chief names used to describe the breed were Rough Highland Greyhound, Highland Greyhound, Wolfdog, and later, Staghound. Indeed, the variety of terms is astonishing, but the most important is the word "Irisch" in this connection. Before the terms Celtic and Highland were known, the

"THE DRUNKARD".

A well-known popular sentimental picture, by Hancock, depicting the unshakeable faithfulness of the Scottish Deerhound.

description Irisch applied equally to Ireland and Scotland, the former country being the better known of the two. Thus in Pitscottie's work we find a description of the inhabitants of Scotland: "They be cloathed with ane mantle, with ane schirt faschioned after the Irisch manner, going bare legged to the knee. All speak Irisch". Holinshed and other writers agree with this evidence, which is significant, because descriptions of Irish Greyhounds about this date (such as occur in Taylor's *Pennilesse Pilgrim*, A.D. 1618) refer without doubt to Highland Greyhounds and not to the great Irish Wolfdog, as has erroneously been supposed. The latter breed had already become so scarce in Ireland in A.D. 1623 that we find the Duke of Buckingham asking for a couple of brace as gifts for princes. At the same period the Earl of Mar could muster, for his deer-drives in Scotland, a couple of hundred "Irish Greyhounds". The Duke of Buckingham would be quite familiar with the Rough Greyhounds used for this purpose, and it is highly unlikely that he would confound them with the all but unique specimens he had caused a search for in Ireland.

Ash, in his great modern work on the Dog, gives an illustration from a book on animals dated A.D. 1583, showing a group containing large Rough Greyhounds, all possessed of such excellence in turn of quarter as to lead one to believe that the picture was made for the express purpose of

Photo]   [Fielder.
FILIAL RESPECT.
A charming study of two of Miss Bransfoot's Deerhounds,
"Rupert" and his son "Bracken of Bransways".

arousing envy in the hearts of all subsequent Deerhound owners. A veritable illustrated counsel of perfection!

There is a record that, at Cowdray Park, Queen Elizabeth saw "sixteen bucks pulled down in a laund", and it is generally supposed that the hounds used were Rough Greyhounds, but just at what point these hounds became peculiarly the pride and possession of Scotland we do not know. All that can be claimed with certainty is that they were long established there before A.D. 1526, and if a graph of Deerhound popularity were made, it would disclose a sustainedly high level for many generations prior to this date, with a sharp decline towards the eighteenth century. Pennant, in 1769, says: "We saw in Gordon Castle a true Highland Greyhound which has become very scarce. It was of large size, strong, deep chested, and covered with very long, rough hair. This kind was in great vogue and used in vast numbers at the magnificent stag chases by powerful chieftains".

These chieftains preserved and prized their hounds with a fanatical

CH. "WULPHILDA".
This Deerhound, once the property of Major C. E. Davis, was a fine blue brindle and one of the best of its day.

133

fervour, and Stewart in his *Buik of Chronicles* recounts the theft by Picts of a dog, romantically described as excelling all others, "so far as into licht the moon does, neara star". This work was a metrical version of Hector Boece's History, A.D. 1526, and continues: "The pictis houndis were nocht of sic speed as scottis houndis, nor yet so gude at need, nor in sic game they were not half so gude, nor of sicpleasures, nor sic pulchritude".

"Scottis" honour was not avenged upon this

harsh, wiry, reddish hair mixed with white". He mentions particularly that they were "formerly used" for deer-hunting.

Between this date and the revival of the breed, around 1830, it became extremely scarce. Several writers went so far as to pronounce Deerhounds extinct as a separate species, because many old strongholds were drawn blank, or, at best, displayed cross-bred, inferior specimens, and the difficulty of communication prevented proper investigation.

Photo]

[*Ralph Robinson.*

"MOINA OF ROTHERWOOD".

Miss Hartley's Deerhound makes a very fine picture and shows the wire coat that protects the dog in the rough country.

occasion until a hundred Picts and sixty of their comrades lay slain upon the field. One of the dogs illustrated in Gesner's *History of Quadrupeds*, A.D. 1560, is a Deerhound, and the drawing is supplied by Henry St. Clair, Dean of Glasgow, whose family is expressly stated to have kept and bred these hounds for many years prior to that date. Bewick (A.D. 1792) indicates the wane of deer-driving in many parts of Scotland, with its inevitable bearing upon the dogs used. He says "One of these dogs which we saw some years ago, was a large, powerful, fierce-looking animal. Its ears were pendulous and its eyes half hid in hair, its body was strong and muscular, and covered with

The breed lived, however, and had its fastidious supporters as engrossed in pedigree and points as many who had gone before, or were yet to adopt its cause.

Rawdon Lee, Cupples, and other well-informed writers, give lists of districts where good and pure-bred hounds still flourished.

Mr. Menzies, of Chesthill, claimed one strain in his family since 1750. Badenoch and Lochaber possessed "adequate supplies", and numerous historians acknowledge a debt of gratitude to the farmers and to some of the clergy along the West coast, and in the islands, for their efforts in preserving the best stock. Dalzell's *Book of the Dog*

Ralph Robinson

HERDWICK SHEEP

Two of Mrs. M. Richardson's Herdwick ewes.

[Photo]   [Ralph Robinson.

ON EXMOOR.

Miss M. Redmond is here seen with some of the good specimens from her kennel on one of the finest moors in England, which provide ideal surroundings for these noble dogs.

mentions Captain Basil Hall's hounds of the Glenmoriston breed, and Mr. Grant had this line at Invermoriston since 1815. He states that his first dog came from Captain Macdonald, of Moray, in the Braes of Lochaber, and the first bitch hailed from that pillar of the breed, Mr. Mackenzie, of Applecross. She was "celebrated for her great courage and lasting power". This list could be still further augmented, and it seems strange, in face of incontrovertible proof to the contrary, that Mr. Scrope, in his contemporary work on deer-stalking, should pronounce the Deerhound almost extinct. Cupples, in *Deerhounds and their Masters*, explains this, however, by the jealousy with which the

more modern history of Deerhounds, when several great kennels have taken little or no part in the continuation of the breed, one at least being completely lost in consequence.

This great wave of renewed interest dated from the rescinding of the Act (1831) whereby the shooting of game had hitherto been reserved for certain ranks and estates. Enthusiasm was instantaneous, and spread rapidly through the Highlands. Deer-driving, as distinguished from stalking, was no longer practised, but from that date onwards the records of the great stalkers of the latter part of the last century give ample evidence of the quality to which the breed was again raised. Fore-

Photo]   *[Fall.*

ALL IN A ROW.

Five of Miss Hartley's kennel. Like all the Greyhound family (for Deerhounds are Rough-haired and large Greyhounds really), they carry their tails in the usual fashion.

breed was now regarded. Rivalry ran high and, history repeating itself, shows instances after 1830 where the purloining of a Deerhound aroused wrath that, if it were not so vengeful, ranked in heat with the fury of ancient "Scottis" days ! We are told, too, that many a Parliamentary vote could be assured by the promise of a single pup !

One kennel is reputed to have resorted to outside stock only three times in a hundred years, and it was the rule with the Earl de Folcoville that no puppy might be preserved beyond the needs of his own forest, excepting as a very rare favour to some stalker in his immediate circle. Cupples likens this attitude to "the man who wished to reserve the enjoyment of Horace for himself and a few friends", and it is a strange coincidence that examples of similar miserliness recur even in the

most in the movement ranks the Colonsay family, whose indefatigable efforts produced splendid results. Of the six sons, the eldest—later Lord Colonsay—and his brother, Mr. Archibald McNeill, took the chief part. They spared no expense, bred extensively, and kept only the best. Lord Henry Bentinck, Mr. Menzies, of Chesthill, and Cameron of Lochiel maintained magnificent strains up to the 'seventies, as did the Duke of Leeds and many others. Crossing was resorted to ; in some instances a single introduction, in others a wider range of experiment prevailed. The controversy which raged around this subject makes interesting reading to-day, when it can be reviewed impartially and examined in the light of ultimate results. But none can fail to respect the purists, who so deeply resented the foreign blood

Photo]   [Walter Guiver.

"MAGNETIC OF ROSS".
The Misses Loughrey's "Magnetic of Ross" the winner of the Challenge Certificate
at the Birmingham Show, 1933.

blood completely, and the appearance of the Deerhound suffered nothing in the long run. Indeed, the verdict of authority has long gone forth proclaiming the outcome a general benefit. In many instances, however, these infusions were a failure, and were not persevered with beyond the initial stage. McNeill himself tells us that the Russian Wolfhound and other big dogs which he imported were never used at all, as he did not find them the equal in fire and courage of the strains he had thought then might improve. The question of crossing, however, and the name of Glengarry, have ever been coupled in Deerhound circles, for he experimented more freely than any other kennel of his day. A slur has rested against the record of this great stalker on this account, which should long since have been dispelled. That Glengarry introduced the Cuban Bloodhound, and, in his efforts to produce a race of trackers, "came near to inventing a new variety", everyone knows, but few remember that he was as fastidious of the true stock as the most conservative among his fellows. Again and again occurs testimony to the fact that "Glengarry possessed the best strains", and, as an instance, Mr. Peter Robertson of the Black Mount Forest, describes his brace, "Glen" and "Garry". thus: "The former nearly 33 inches, the bitch 30 inches, both rough, lightish - grey, and they were perfectly pure, would not track a deer, but ran by sight only, and we thought much of them, as would be supposed".

Writing of the day upon which Glengarry met his death in the tragedy of Loch Linnhe, his old head-keeper said: "There was a leash of his best along with him in the steamer at the time, 'Truelais', and she was as good a tracker as ever ran, and 'Comstrie', who was thoroughbred, the best that ever I saw of any kind, and I am eighty-six years of age and the most part of that time with Glengarry". (Letter, 1876-77).

introduced into many strongholds of the breed. It should, however, be borne in mind that these infusions were resorted to for the improvement of working ability only, and never to alter the characteristics of the race. First crosses are invariably hideous, but four generations will absorb the fresh

The introduction of the express rifle, the division of the great forests into numerous smaller ranges,

Photo]   [Fall.

CH. "DRAMATIC OF ROSS"
This dog. a champion of the Deerhound family, was well-known at all shows.
The words "Of Ross" explain the breeding.

138

THE DEERHOUND.

The harsh strength of the coat, the gentleness of the dark brown eye, the rose-leaf ear and the fine long lines of the muzzle—prominent features of the Deerhound— are here well portrayed.

By Ernest G. Chesson.

139

and other causes led to the final disuse of the Deerhound in its native land. Time works many changes, and it is a far cry from the great drives of the sixteenth century to the humble Collie on a string that is all the stalker of to-day requires for his sport, when the avoidance of anything likely to disturb the forest is a point of first importance. The advent of dog shows in 1861 was therefore a fortunate occurrence for Deerhounds, and many of the great sportsmen sent their cracks to these exhibitions. In the list of winning owners for a number of years, one reads a sequence of names which recall the great days that were then drawing to a close. The Duke of Sutherland, Lord Henry Bentinck, Sir St. George Gore, Cameron of Lochiel, Mr. Menzies, of Chesthill, Sir John McNeil—all of whom bred for perfection both in work and appearance, and sent entries straight from the hill to Curzon Hall. From this stock is descended all the hounds existing at the present day. Colonel Inge, of Thorpe, had the honour of winning the first prize at the first show (in Birmingham, 1861), with a dog called "Valiant". This dog's pedigree was given as by Lord Saltoun's famous "Bran", out of "Seaforth's Vengeance". "Bran" was entered to his first stag at nine months old, and killed his last at nine years. His greatest exploit in a marvellous career was the killing of two unwounded stags single-handed in three-quarters of an hour. He was at his best about 1844-45.

The great dog of the 'sixties was Mr. Gillespie's "Torrom", described as "a steel-grey, not very

A DEERHOUND PUPPY.
This daughter of "Rupert" is "Coronach of Bransways", at the age of four and a half months. Notice the type of head. She was bred by Miss Branfoot.

high but remarkably well formed". Captain Graham mentions (1881) that "all dogs of any note at the present time could trace their descent from this exceedingly grand specimen". From a dog called "Grumach", of the strain belonging to Mr. Campbell, of Monzie, "Lochiel's Pirate" was bred. This dog, together with his litter brother, Ch. "Old Torrom", was pupped in 1866, the former a remarkably fine specimen. The latter, an extraordinarily heavy dog of medium brownish colour, had little to recommend him, and is not to be confounded with his famous grandsire, "Gillespie's Torrom". Of a different

FRIENDS.
There is no more docile breed than the Deerhound, and here we have a youngster with its little mistress. Though good pets, this breed needs plenty of exercise.

140

Photo] [*Ralph Robinson.*

THE DEATH.

In the present century all Greyhound breeds have been tried at coursing. Deerhounds, although really too large for coursing hares are, nevertheless, occasionally used quite successfully.

strain, going direct back to McNeill's dogs, stands "Hector", the property of Mr. Dadley, head-keeper to the Marquis of Bristol, one which was considered a truly splendid specimen. Of a good rough coat, darkish brindle in colour, by "Giaour" out of "Hylda", he stood 31 inches, girthed 35 inches, and weighed 105 lb. This dog was a grandson of "Keildar", bred by Mr. Cole, head-keeper at Windsor Park, and at whose death he was acquired by Captain Graham. According to authorities, "Keildar" was one of the most elegant and aristocratic dogs ever seen. He stood "full 30 inches, girthed 33½. and weighed 95 lb."

On the death of General Ross, of Glenmordart, his hounds passed to Major Robertson, and from "Oscar" and "Hilda" he bred "Morni", perhaps the greatest name in the history of the breed. This dog came into the hands of Mr. Hickman, and is confidently described as combining all the graces. He passed on his good points, and Cameron of Lochiel describes his grandson, "Lord of the Isles", as "beyond criticism". The only litter got by this dog contained Ch. "Fingal II" (bred by Mr. Hickman), which was acquired by Mr. Walter Evans. Another great dog, born the same year (1884), was Mr. Morse Goulter's Ch. "Atholl II". These two dominant sires form the tap-roots of the modern breed. The former bred Ch. "Earl II", the latter Ch. "Swift".

Another great kennel about this era sponsored a heavier type of hound, and with stock gathered from Fort Augustus and elsewhere, Mrs. Grew made tremendous inroads on the prize-money for many years. The two schools of thought were definitely opposed, but many of her best hounds are spoken of by the apostles of grace and symmetry in terms of high praise. Ch. "Ayrshire", Ch. "Forester", Ch. "Kelso", three of her great stars, are now incorporated with the lines of "Fingal" and "Atholl", and have in turn produced some notable stock. To mention but a few more of the most remarkable inmates of important kennels, Mr. Hood Wright's celebrity, Ch. "Selwood Morven", sold to Mr. Harry Rawson, held a great position

in the 'nineties. This owner's Ch. "St. Ronan's Ranger" (bred by Mr. W. Martin) proved to be one of the most successful sires some years later, and Ch. "St. Ronan's Rhyme" (the result of chance mating at nine months old) holds the record of the greatest show career of any bitch in the breed. Mrs. Armstrong's Ch. "Rob Roy of Abbotsford", another much used and successful sire, produced a large percentage of winners before the war. No record of the breed, however, could be complete without mention of the service rendered by Sir Henry MacLaughlin, whose enthusiasm in Ireland resulted in a nucleus of well-bred dogs there which have since resulted in the salvation of the breed.

Like all other big breeds, the period immediately following the Armistice proved a hazardous one for Deerhounds. However, "Duich of Springfort", an Irish-bred hound, born in the restricted era, was found near Dublin, and proved an immediate success at stud. Himself the sire of three champions, his son, Ch. "Tragic of Ross", may be said to have restored the breed to its pre-war eminence.

STANDARD OF THE DEERHOUND.

HEAD. — The head should be broadest at the ears, tapering slightly to the eyes, with the muzzle tapering more decidedly to the nose. The muzzle should be pointed, but the teeth and lips level. The head should be long ; the skull flat, rather than round, with a very slight rise over the eyes, but with nothing approaching a stop. The skull should be coated with moderately long hair, which is softer than the rest of the coat. The nose should be black (though in some blue-fawns the colour is blue) and slightly aquiline. In the lighter-coloured dogs a black muzzle is preferred. There should be a good moustache of rather silky hair, and a fair beard.

EARS.—The ears should be set on high and, in repose, folded back like the Greyhounds, though raised above the head in excitement without losing the fold, and even in some cases semierect. A prick ear is bad. A big, thick ear, hanging flat to the head or heavily coated with long hair, is the worst of faults. The ear should be

[Photo]   [Sport and General.

ON THE ALERT.

The Misses Longtrey's "Idric of Ross" and Ch. "Thorp of the Foothills" at Cruft's International Show in 1924.   The latter won first prize and was the best Deerhound in the show.

143

soft, glossy, and like a mouse's coat to the touch ; the smaller it is the better. It should have no long coat or long fringe, but there is often a silky, silvery coat on the body of the ear and the tip. Whatever the general colour, the ears should be black or dark-coloured.

NECK AND SHOULDERS.—The neck should be long —that is, of the length that befits the Greyhound character of the dog. An over-long neck is not necessary nor desirable, for the dog is not required to stoop to his work like a Greyhound, and it must be remembered that the mane, which every good specimen should have, detracts from the apparent length of neck. Moreover, a Deerhound requires a very strong neck to hold a stag. The nape of the neck should be very prominent where the head is set on, and the throat should be clean cut at the angle, and prominent. The shoulder should be well sloped, the blades well back and not too much width between them. Loaded and straight shoulders are very bad faults.

TAIL.—Should be tolerably long, tapering, and reaching to within about $1\frac{1}{2}$ inches off the ground. When the dog is still, dropped perfectly straight down, or curved. When in motion, it should be curved when excited, but in no case to be lifted out of the line of the back. It should be well covered with hair on the inside, thick and wiry, underside longer, and towards the end a slight fringe not objectionable. A curl or ring tail is very undesirable.

EYES.—The eyes should be dark ; generally speaking, they are dark-brown or hazel. A very light eye is not liked. The eye is moderately full, with a soft look in repose, but a keen, far-away look when the dog is roused. The rims of the eyelids should be black.

BODY.—The body and general formation is that of a Greyhound of larger size and bone. Chest, deep rather than broad, but not too narrow and flat-sided. The loins well arched, and drooping to the tail. A straight back is not desirable, this formation being unsuitable for going up-hill, and very unsightly.

LEGS AND FEET.—The legs should be broad and flat, and good broad forearm and elbow being desirable. Forelegs, of course, as straight as

Photo] "REVIS OF ROTHERWOOD". [Fall.
A nicely bred Deerhound, one of Miss Hartley's kennel, standing well at attention.

possible. Feet close and compact, with well-arranged toes. The hindquarters drooping and as broad and powerful as possible, the hips being set wide apart. The hindlegs should be well bent at the stifle, with great length from the hip to the hock, which should be broad and flat. Cow-hocks, weak pasterns, straight stifles and splay feet are very bad faults.

COAT.—The hair on the body, neck, and quarters should be harsh and wiry and about three or four inches long ; that on the head, breast and belly is much softer. There should be a slight hairy fringe on the inside of the fore- and hindlegs, but nothing approaching the "feather" of the Collie. The Deerhound should be a shaggy dog, but not over-coated. A woolly coat is bad. Some good strains have a mixture of silky coat with the hard, which is preferable to a woolly coat ; but the proper coat is a thick, close-lying, ragged coat, harsh or crisp to the touch.

COLOUR.—Colour is much a matter of fancy. But there is no manner of doubt that the dark blue-grey is the most preferred. Next comes the darker and lighter greys or brindles (the darkest being generally preferred), yellow and sandy-red or red-fawn, especially with black points, i.e. ears and muzzles are also in equal estimation, this being the colour of the oldest known strains— the McNeill and Chesthill Menzies. White is condemned by all the old authorities, but a white chest and white toes, occurring as they do in a great many of the darkest-coloured dogs, are not so greatly objected to, but the less the better, as the Deerhound is a self-coloured dog. A white blaze on the head or a white collar should entirely disqualify. In other cases, though passable, yet an attempt should be made to get rid of white markings. The less white the better, but a slight white tip to the stern occurs in the best strains.

HEIGHT of dogs should be not less than 30 inches, or even more if there be symmetry without coarseness. Height of bitches, 28 inches upwards. There can be no objection to a bitch being large, unless too coarse, as even at her greatest height

144

CH. "AETHETIC OF ROSS".
The Misses M. F. and H. M. Loughrey, of Ireland, are two leading owners of Deerhounds. Ch. "Aethetic of Ross" is a very good type.

CH. "PADRAIC OF ROSS".
A good picture of this well-built Deerhound, showing clearly the desired type. He is one of the Misses Loughrey's kennel.

145

she does not approach that of the dog, and, therefore, could not have been too big for work, as over-big dogs are. Besides, a big bitch is good for breeding and keeping up the size.

WEIGHT.—From 80 to 105 lb.

THE FAMILY.

A very unusual picture indeed showing a deerhound mother with two of her puppies, the property of Miss Bishment. The parent seems to be very proud indeed of her family.

Photo] "RUPERT OF TROTTISCLIFFE". *[Fall.*

Miss E. S. M. Branfoot, of Bransways, the well-known breeder of Bedlingtons, also specializes in Deerhounds.
Here is a distinguished member of her kennel.

148

"EUAM OF BRIDGE SOLLERS".
Miss E. M. R. Reoch is a breeder of Deerhounds, the old breed from which the Irish Wolfhounds were developed.

A WINNING TEAM.
he three Deerhounds shown here are Ch. "Bran of Bridge Sollers", with "Hector" and
"Solomon", all of the famous Bridge Sollers breed.

DEERHOUND HEADS.

The Rough-haired Greyhound of the North goes well with the scenery of its native home. Here is a head study of two of Miss Lynton's kennel.

CH. "PHORP OF THE FOOTHILLS".

A head study of this well-known champion, the property of the Misses Loughrey.

Photo]   ON GUARD.   *[Ralph Robinson.*

Two handsome representatives of Miss Richmond's Deerhound Kennel are seen in the wild country of the moors, very similar to certain parts of Scotland.

this disease, and he was in very good bodily condition, although he had been affected for six weeks. Very soon afterwards, however, an obstinate diarrhoea, with occasional vomiting, set in, and as all kinds of treatment appeared to have no salutary effect, the

some amount of observation of the patient during twenty-four or more hours, combined, of course, with the performance of all forms of clinical enquiry. Many of the canine, agricultural, and society journals have their veterinary advice columns, to which readers

CHARACTERISTICS.

Miss R. Branfoot is not only a well-known breeder of Deerhounds, but also a clever artist. She has made these drawings specially for this Encyclopaedia. They depict these fascinating Hounds in all sorts of characteristic moods and attitudes.

AFTER EVERY CHASE.

(In the old frontiersmanl in company with his motorboard companion, returning their field re which is a glowing characteristic of both dogs. They have found their wood master after the Indians settle, and who are the stealth approach when eyes are as expressive. This fine painting is by H. Oskee, and hangs in beautiful Manor Nebraska.)

CH. "ST. RONAN'S RHYME."

In Deerhound history this excellent specimen has an outstanding place. It was bred and shown by Mr. Harry Rawson and was claimed to be the greatest winning bitch.

(The Messrs F. M. and H. M. Company)

THE DEERHOUND   PADDY PROMISE OF BRANSWAYS

ALTHOUGH somewhat similar to an Irish Wolfhound, this breed is a far older one and is built on finer lines, somewhat heavier than a Greyhound but with a rough coat.

The dog is sometimes referred to as a Rough-coated Greyhound. Its stance and general characteristics certainly lend support to the suggestion.

One thing, however, is quite certain—that the dog has been known in the Highlands of Scotland for many centuries, where it was used for hunting the deer and stag.

Like many other dogs of its type, plenty of open space is needed to ensure exercise.

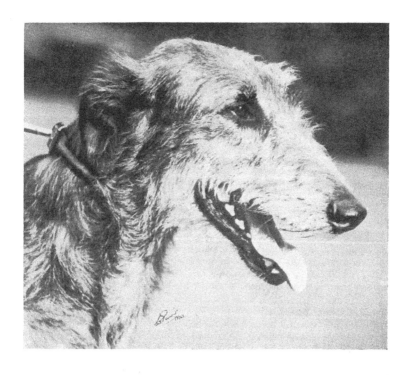

THE DEERHOUND   PADDY PROMISE OF BRANSWAYS

THE DEERHOUND

HEAD : The head should be broadest at the ears, tapering slightly to the eyes, with the muzzle tapering more decidedly to the nose. The muzzle should be pointed, but the teeth and lips level. The head should be long, the skull flat rather than round, with a very slight rise over the eyes, but with nothing approaching a stop. The skull should be coated with moderately long hair, which is softer than the rest of the coat. The nose should be black (though in some blue-fawns the colour is blue), and slightly aquiline. In the lighter-coloured dogs a black muzzle is preferred. There should be a good moustache of rather silky hair, and a fair beard.

EARS : The ears should be set on high, and, in repose, folded back like the Greyhound's, though raised above the head in excitement without losing the fold, and even in some cases semi-erect. A prick ear is bad. A big thick ear hanging flat to the head, or heavily coated with long hair, is the worst of faults. The ear should be soft, glossy, and like a mouse's coat to the touch, and the smaller it is the better. It should have no long coat or long fringe, but there is often a silky silvery coat on the body of the ear and the tip. Whatever the general colour, the ears should be black or dark-coloured.

EYES : The eyes should be dark ; generally they are dark brown or hazel. A very light eye is not liked. The eye is moderately full, with a soft look in repose, but a keen, far-away look when the dog is roused. The rims of the eyelids should be black.

BODY : The body and general formation is that of a greyhound of larger size and bone. Chest deep rather than broad, but not too narrow and flat-sided. The loin well arched and drooping to the tail. A straight back is not desirable, this formation being unsuitable for going uphill, and very unsightly.

NECK AND SHOULDERS : The neck should be long—that is, of the length that befits the Greyhound character of the dog. An over-long neck is not necessary nor desirable, for the dog is not required to stoop to his work like a Greyhound, and it must be remembered that the mane, which every good specimen should have, detracts from the apparent length of neck. Moreover, a Deerhound requires a very strong neck to hold a stag. The nape of the neck should be very prominent where the head is set on, and the throat should be clean cut at the angle and prominent. The shoulders should be well sloped, the blades well back and not too much width between them. Loaded and straight shoulders very bad faults.

LEGS AND FEET : The legs should be broad and flat, and good broad forearm and elbow being desirable. Forelegs, of course, as straight as possible. Feet close and compact, with well arranged toes. The hindquarters drooping, and as broad as powerful as possible, the hips being set wide apart. The hindlegs should be well bent at the stifle, with great length from the hip to the hock, which should be broad and flat. Cowhocks, weak pasterns, straight stifles, and splay feet very bad faults.

TAIL : Tail should be tolerably long, tapering, and reaching to within about 1½ inches off the ground. When the dog is still, dropped perfectly straight down, or curved. When in motion it should be curved when excited, in no case to be lifted out of the line of the back. It should be well covered with hair, on the inside, thick and wiry, underside longer, and towards the end a slight fringe not objectionable. A curl or ring tail very undesirable.

COAT : The hair on the body, neck and quarters should be harsh and wiry, and about three or four inches long ; that on the head, breast and belly is much softer. There should be a slight hairy fringe on the inside of the fore and hind legs, but nothing approaching the " feather " of a colley. The Deerhound should be a shaggy dog, but not over-coated. A woolly coat is bad. Some good strains have a mixture of silky coat with the hard, which is preferable to a woolly coat ; but the proper coat is a thick, close-lying, ragged coat, harsh or crisp to the touch.

COLOUR : Colour is much a matter of fancy. But there is no manner of doubt that the dark blue-grey is the most preferred. Next comes the darker and lighter greys or brindles, the darkest being generally preferred. Yellow and sandy red or red fawn, especially with black points, i.e., ears and muzzles are also in equal estimation, this being the colour of the oldest known strains, the M'Neil and Chesthill Menzies. White is condemned by all the old authorities, but a white chest and white toes, occurring as they do in a great many of the darkest-coloured dogs, are not so greatly objected to, but the less the better, as the Deerhound is a self-coloured dog. A white blaze on the head, or a white collar, should entirely disqualify. In other cases, though passable, yet an attempt should be made to get rid of white markings. The less white the better, but a slight white tip to the stern occurs in the best strains.

HEIGHT OF DOGS : From 28 to 30 inches, or even more if there be symmetry without coarseness, but which is rare.

HEIGHT OF BITCHES : From 26 inches upwards. There can be no objection to a bitch being large, unless too coarse, as even at her greatest height she does not approach that of the dog, and therefore, could not have been too big for work, as over-big dogs are. Besides, a big bitch is good for breeding and keeping up the size.

WEIGHT : From 85 to 105 lbs. in dogs and from 65 to 80 lbs. in bitches.

The above description was drawn up by Messrs. Hickman and R. Hood Wright, arranged and finally approved at a meeting of the Club, November 26th, 1892, and endorsed at the meeting of the Club, June, 1901, at Shrewsbury.

NOTE.—The average height of Deerhounds has increased since the foregoing standard was drawn up, and although hounds of the heights mentioned are quite eligible for competition, it is desirable that dogs should be not less than 30 inches, and bitches 28 inches, at the shoulder, respectively.

STANDARD OF POINTS

1. Typical. A Deerhound should resemble a rough-coated Greyhound of larger size and bone.
2. Movements easy, active and true.
3. As tall as possible consistent with quality.
4. Head—long, level, well balanced, carried high.
5. Body—long, very deep in brisket, well sprung ribs and great breadth across hips.
6. Forelegs—strong and quite straight, with elbows neither in nor out.
7. Thighs—long and muscular, second thighs well muscled, stifles nicely bent.
8. Loins—well arched, and belly well drawn up.

9. Coat—rough and hard, longer and softer beard and brows.
10. Feet—close and compact, with well knuckled toes.
11. Ears—small, with Greyhound like carriage.
12. Eyes—dark, moderately full.
13. Neck—long, well arched, and very strong, with prominent nape.
14. Shoulders—clean, set sloping.
15. Chest—very deep, but not too narrow.
16. Tail—long and slightly curbed, carried low.
17. Teeth—strong and level.
18. Nails—strong and curved.

DEERHOUND
By Sir Edwin Landseer

Lightning Source UK Ltd.
Milton Keynes UK
UKHW011652190821
389122UK00002B/422